Finance for Freelancers

Maximize Income, Manage Cash Flow, Minimize Stress

Veronica Goldspiel

Copyright© 2024 Veronica Goldspiel

All rights reserved.

All rights reserved. No part of this publication may be reproduced, distributed, or transmitted in any form or by any means, including photocopying, recording, or other electronic or mechanical methods, or by any information storage and retrieval system without prior written permission of the publisher, except in the case of very brief quotations embodied in critical reviews and certain other noncommercial uses permitted by copyright law.

This book is designed to provide accurate and authoritative information regarding the subject matter herein. It is sold with the understanding that the author and publisher are not engaged in rendering legal, accounting, or other professional services. If you require legal advice or other expert assistance, you should seek the services of a competent professional.

While the author has made every effort to provide accurate website addresses and other information at the time of publication, neither the publisher nor the author assumes any responsibility for errors or changes that occur after publication. Further, the publisher does not have any control over and does not assume any responsibility for author or third-party websites or their content.

Book Cover by Veronica Goldspiel

1st Edition 2024

ISBN: 979-8-9903604-4-0 (Paperback)

Disclaimer

This publication is designed to provide accurate and authoritative information with regard to the subject matter covered. It is sold with the understanding that the publisher is not engaged in rendering legal, accounting, or other professional advice. If legal advice or other expert assistance is required, the services of a competent professional should be sought.

The author wishes to acknowledge the respective sources for use of graphs, charts, and other data in this book, and it is the author's intent to portray that data accurately rather than through representations.

This book may contain technical or other errors. Veronica Goldspiel and GCE Publishing do not guarantee its accuracy, completeness, or suitability. In no event shall Veronica Goldspiel and GCE Publishing be liable for any special, indirect, or consequential damages relating to this material for any use of this material or for any referenced website and courses, or the application of any idea or strategy in this book.

The information contained in this book is provided by Veronica Goldspiel and GCE Publishing, and it is offered for educational and informational purposes only. Veronica Goldspiel is a not a licensed financial planner. She suggests that you consult with a qualified legal or tax-planning professional with regard to your personal circumstances. Nothing in this book should be interpreted or construed as legal, regulatory, insurance, tax, or financial planning advice or as an offer to perform services related to any of these fields in any respect.

The content of this book contains general information and may not reflect current legal, tax, insurance, or regulatory developments and information, and it is not guaranteed to be correct, complete, or current. Veronica Goldspiel and GCE Publishing make no warranty, expressed or implied, as to the accuracy or reliability of this information or the information contained in any referenced website or course.

Readers of this book should not act or refrain from acting on the basis of any information included herein without seeking appropriate legal or other relevant advice related to the particular facts and circumstances at issue from an attorney or other advisor duly and properly licensed in the recipient's state of residence. Veronica Goldspiel and GCE Publishing expressly disclaim all liability with respect to actions taken or not taken by the reader based on any or all of the information or other contents within this book or provided by Veronica Goldspiel directly. Any information sent to Veronica Goldspiel or GCE Publishing via Internet, e-mail, or through any referenced website is not secure and is done so on a non-confidential basis.

Should the reader of this book seek a referral to any service provider, the person to whom such referral is made is solely responsible for assessing the knowledge, skill, or capabilities of such provider, and neither the author, presenter, nor Veronica Goldspiel, GCE Publishing are responsible for the quality, integrity, performance, or any other aspect of any services ultimately provided by such provider or any damages, consequential or incidental, arising from the use of such provider. Any opinions expressed in the book are mine alone and mine based on the information publicly available to me in my interpretation of that information.

FREE GIFTS JUST FOR YOU!

I've created some FREE GIFTS just for readers of this book. This FREE content contains some resources to help you more easily learn, grow, and succeed in your freelance career!

- **Freelancer's Resource & Tools Guide** – This is my list of books, audio, websites, and more to assist you in reaching your ultimate freelance career dreams.

- **The Freelancer's Life Private Facebook Group**: A vibrant community where freelancers unite to share insights, gain support, and elevate their careers. Whether you're just starting out or are a seasoned pro, join us to connect with like-minded professionals, discover success strategies, and thrive in your freelance journey. This is your space to learn, grow, and succeed together!

GET YOUR FREE GIFT NOW BY GOING TO:

https://goldspielcreativeenterprises.com/free-gifts-freelancer-success-sign-up/

CONNECT WITH ME ON FACEBOOK!

Join my *The Freelancer's Life* private Facebook community here:

https://www.facebook.com/groups/thefreelancerslife

Contents

INTRODUCTION	1
Chapter 1: The Power of Financial Goals – Your Freelance Compass to Success	3
Chapter 2: Master Your Vision: Designing a Business Plan for Growth	7
Chapter 3: Fueling Your Freedom: Crafting a Smart Budget for Your Freelance Business	13
Chapter 4: The Art of Money Mapping: Tracking Your Income and Expenses	19
Chapter 5: The Importance of Keeping Personal and Business Finances Separate	25
Chapter 6: Setting Clear Payment Terms	31
Chapter 7: The Art of the Invoice	37
Chapter 8: Don't Put All Your Eggs in One Basket	43
Chapter 9: Saving for Taxes	49
Chapter 10: Planning for Slow Periods	55
Chapter 11: Keeping Your Finger on the Pulse of Industry Trends	61
Chapter 12: The Freelancer's Tax Treasure Hunt	67
Chapter 13: The Fine Print Finesse	73
Chapter 14: Your Financial GPS – Why Every Freelancer Needs a Financial Advisor	79
Chapter 15: Reviewing Your Financial Goals Annually	85
Chapter 16: Building a Buffer for Life's Freelance Surprises	89

Chapter 17: Automating Savings (Even When Your Income is Wild)	93
Chapter 18: From Gig to Golden Years	99
Chapter 19: Freelance Perks: Crafting Your Own Benefits Plan	105
Chapter 20: Keeping Debt in Check	111
Chapter 21: Big Dreams, Bigger Purchases	117
Chapter 22: Investing in Your Success	123
Chapter 23: Profit Tune-Up: How to Keep Your Rates Aligned With Your Value	131
Chapter 24: Keeping the Momentum Going	137
Chapter 25: Smart Financial Tools for Freelancers	143
CONCLUSION	151
PLEASE DO ME A HUGE FAVOR	153
REMINDER	155
ABOUT THE AUTHOR	157
OTHER BOOKS BY AUTHOR	159

INTRODUCTION

> *"All you need is the plan, the road map, and the courage to press on to your destination."* -Earl Nightingale

Welcome to *Finance for Freelancers: Maximize Income, Manage Cash Flow, Minimize Stress*! If you're reading this, you're either considering diving into the exciting world of freelancing or you've already taken the plunge and are looking for ways to make your freelance business not only survive but thrive. Wherever you are on your freelance journey, this book is here to guide you, inspire you, and help you take control of your finances so you can focus on what you do best: offering your unique skills to the world.

Let me start with a confession. When I began freelancing almost two decades ago, I had absolutely no idea what I was doing. In fact, I didn't even realize I was a freelancer! I was taking on projects, completing them, and moving on to the next without any real structure or understanding of how to run a freelance business. It took me several years to figure out that what I was doing was, in fact, freelancing. And even longer to truly understand the intricacies that come with running a successful freelance operation.

I've had the incredible opportunity to work with some of the top motivational speakers in the world – people like Tony Robbins, T. Harv Eker, Jordan Belfort, Pam Hendrickson, and others. But my path to success wasn't a straight line. I learned a lot of things the hard way. From managing my cash flow to setting the right rates, I made mistakes, hit roadblocks, and faced my share of financial stress. And that's exactly why I wrote this book – so you don't have to go through the same struggles.

Whether you're just starting out or have been freelancing for a while, this book is designed to help you either set yourself up for success or streamline and optimize the business you've already built. Freelancing can be incredibly rewarding, but it also comes with its own set of challenges – especially when it comes to managing money. That's why I'm going to walk you through practical strategies for maximizing your income, keeping your cash flow steady, and, perhaps most importantly, reducing the financial stress that often comes with running your own business.

Now, you'll notice that throughout this book, I'll be repeating some key strategies and concepts in various chapters. This isn't accidental. These principles are interconnected and are foundational to your freelance success. They don't just apply to one area of your business – they impact everything. And these strategies aren't "one and done." You can't just set it and forget it. You'll need to reevaluate, revise, and adapt as your business grows and evolves.

Freelancing is a dynamic journey, full of twists and turns. Your goals will change. Your clients will change. Your income will fluctuate. But with the tools and insights in this book, you'll have a solid foundation to not only navigate the ups and downs but thrive through them.

So, if you're ready to take charge of your freelance finances, maximize your income, and finally eliminate the stress that keeps you up at night, then keep reading. I'm excited to share what I've learned with you, and I can't wait to see how your freelance business transforms!

Chapter 1: The Power of Financial Goals – Your Freelance Compass to Success

*"**D**on't get distracted. Never tell yourself that you need to be the biggest brand in the whole world. Start by working on what you need at the present moment and then what you need to do tomorrow. So, set yourself manageable targets."* -Jas Bagniewski, founder and CEO of Eve Mattress

As a freelancer, you're the captain of your own ship, sailing the vast, often unpredictable waters of the freelance world. But without a compass, even the most skilled captain can lose their way. That compass? It's your financial goals. Setting financial goals isn't just important; it's essential. It's what transforms your freelance business from a passion project into a sustainable, thriving enterprise.

Why Setting Financial Goals is Crucial for Freelancers

Imagine setting out on a road trip without a destination in mind. Sure, the journey might be fun for a while, but sooner or later, you'll find yourself lost, running out of fuel, and wondering where you're going. That's what freelancing can feel like without clear financial goals. Here's why they're so crucial:

Direction and Focus: Financial goals give you a clear direction. Instead of just taking on any project that comes your way, you can focus on the ones that align with your goals. Want to save for a down payment on a house? Knowing that figure will motivate you to seek higher-paying clients or increase your rates.

Motivation: Freelancing can be tough, with its fair share of highs and lows. But having financial goals can keep you motivated. When you know what you're working towards – whether it's a dream vacation, financial independence, or just paying off debt – you'll push through those tough days with a clear sense of purpose.

Financial Stability: Without financial goals, it's easy to fall into a feast-or-famine cycle. You might make a lot of money one month and barely scrape by the next. Setting financial goals help you smooth out those ups and downs by planning for the future, saving for lean times, and ensuring you're charging what you're worth.

Professional Growth: Financial goals aren't just about the money. They're about growth. By setting goals, you're pushing yourself to take on bigger projects, learn new skills, and expand your business. This growth translates into more opportunities, higher income, and greater job satisfaction.

Peace of Mind: Let's face it – financial stress is a huge burden. But when you have clear financial goals and a plan to achieve them, that stress diminishes. You'll sleep better at night knowing you're on track to meet your needs and wants, with a safety net in place for unexpected expenses.

Practical Steps to Set Financial Goals as a Freelancer

Now that we've established why financial goals are essential, let's dive into the how. Setting financial goals might seem daunting, especially when income can be unpredictable. But fear not – here's a step-by-step guide to setting financial goals that are achievable, realistic, and tailored to your freelance life.

Start with the Big Picture: Think about your long-term vision. Where do you see yourself in five, ten, or even twenty years? Do you want to own a home? Retire early? Travel the world? Write down these big-picture dreams – they'll be the foundation for your financial goals.

Break It Down: Once you have your long-term vision, break it down into smaller, manageable goals. For example, if your goal is to buy a house in five years, break it down into yearly savings targets. This makes big goals feel less overwhelming and more achievable.

Make Them SMART: You've probably heard of SMART goals – Specific, Measurable, Achievable, Relevant, and Time-Bound. I wrote about these types of goals in detail in my book, *Dream Catchers*. Applying this framework to your financial goals ensures they're clear and actionable. Instead of saying, *"I want to save more money,"* say, *"I will save $10,000 by the end of the year by setting aside $833 each month."*

Prioritize Your Goals: Not all goals are created equal. Some are more urgent or important than others. Prioritize your goals based on your needs and desires. For example, building an emergency fund might take precedence over saving for a vacation.

Create a Plan: Goals without a plan are just wishes. Once you've set your financial goals, create a plan to achieve them. This could involve setting up automatic transfers to a savings account, increasing your rates, or taking on additional projects. Break down the steps you need to take and make them part of your daily, weekly, or monthly routine.

Track Your Progress: There's nothing more satisfying than seeing your progress. Use a spreadsheet, app, or even a simple notebook to track your progress toward each goal. Celebrate the small wins along the way – each step forward is a victory!

Adjust as Needed: Life happens. Maybe a big project falls through, or you have unexpected expenses. Don't be afraid to adjust your goals if needed. The key is to stay flexible and keep moving forward, even if it means altering your plan.

Tips and Tricks for Setting (and Sticking to) Financial Goals

Setting financial goals is one thing – sticking to them is another. Here are some tips and tricks to keep you on track:

1. **Visualize Your Goals:** Create a vision board or write down your goals and put them somewhere you'll see them every day. Visualization is a powerful tool for keeping your goals front and center in your mind.

2. **Accountability Partners:** Share your goals with a trusted friend, mentor, or fellow freelancer. Having someone to check in with can provide accountability and encouragement, especially during tough times.

3. **Automate Where Possible:** Set up automatic transfers to your savings or investment accounts. This way, you're consistently working towards your goals without even thinking about it. Out of sight, out of mind – but in a good way!

4. **Reward Yourself:** Setting goals shouldn't feel like punishment. Reward yourself for hitting milestones, even if it's something small like a coffee from your favorite café. These rewards keep you motivated and make the journey more enjoyable.

5. **Mind Your Mindset:** A positive mindset is crucial. Instead of thinking, "I can't afford this," reframe it to, "How can I afford this?" This shift in thinking opens up possibilities and solutions you might not have considered.

6. **Stay Informed:** Financial literacy is key to achieving your goals. Take the time to educate yourself about budgeting, investing, and other financial topics. The more you know, the better equipped you'll be to make smart financial decisions.

7. **Celebrate the Journey:** Remember that success isn't just about the destination – it's about the journey. Celebrate each step you take towards your goals, and appreciate the growth and learning that comes with it.

Conclusion

Setting financial goals is more than just a smart business move – it's the key to freelance freedom. With clear goals in place, you'll navigate the unpredictable waters of freelancing with confidence, knowing you're on track to achieve your dreams. Whether you're saving for a rainy day, investing in your future, or building the freelance business of your dreams, financial goals are the compass that will guide you every step of the way.

So grab that metaphorical map, set your sights on your destination, and start charting your course. The journey might be challenging at times, but with your financial goals in place, you'll find that the rewards are more than worth it. Here's to your financial success, and the freedom that comes with it!

Chapter 2: Master Your Vision: Designing a Business Plan for Growth

> *"If you're in the world of business, that means you're in the business of making money."* -Stephen A. Smith

In the world of freelancing, where the only constant is change, a solid business plan is like a sturdy anchor in a storm. It's your roadmap, your guiding star, and your safety net all rolled into one. Without it, you might find yourself adrift, chasing after every opportunity that comes your way without a clear sense of direction. But with a business plan in hand, you'll navigate the freelance seas with confidence, purpose, and a clear vision of where you're headed.

Why Creating a Business Plan is Essential for Freelancers

You might be thinking, "I'm just one person – do I really need a business plan?" The answer is a resounding yes! A business plan isn't just for big corporations; it's a vital tool for freelancers too. Here's why:

Clarifies Your Vision: A business plan forces you to think deeply about your freelance business. What are your goals? Who are your clients? What services do you offer? Writing it all down brings clarity and focus, turning vague ideas into a concrete vision.

Sets the Foundation: Your business plan is the foundation upon which your freelance business is built. It outlines your mission, your target market, your pricing strategy, and your growth plans. With this foundation in place, you can make informed decisions that align with your long-term goals.

Attracts Clients and Partners: A well-crafted business plan can help you attract the right clients and partners. It shows that you're serious about your business and have a clear plan for success. Whether you're pitching to a potential client or seeking a collaboration, a business plan demonstrates your professionalism and commitment.

Guides Your Financial Strategy: A business plan includes your financial goals and projections, helping you plan for expenses, set pricing, and manage cash flow. It's a crucial tool for ensuring that your freelance business is financially sustainable.

Adapts to Change: The freelance landscape is constantly evolving, and so is your business. A business plan isn't set in stone; it's a living document that you can adjust as needed. Whether you're pivoting to a new market or expanding your services, your business plan will help you navigate those changes with ease.

Keeps You Accountable: With a business plan, you have a clear set of goals and milestones to work towards. It's like having a personal coach keeping you accountable and on track. When distractions arise or motivation wanes, your business plan will remind you of your bigger picture and keep you focused.

Practical Steps to Create a Business Plan as a Freelancer

So, how do you go about creating a business plan that's both practical and inspiring? It's easier than you might think. Here's a step-by-step guide to crafting a business plan that will set you up for freelance success.

1. **Start with Your Mission Statement:** Your mission statement is the heart of your business plan. It's a brief, powerful statement that defines what you do, who you serve, and why you do it. Think of it as your North Star – a guiding light that keeps you aligned with your values and goals. Take some time to reflect on your purpose as a freelancer and distill it into a clear, concise mission statement.

2. **Define Your Target Market:** Who are your ideal clients? What problems do

they need solving? Understanding your target market is crucial for tailoring your services, pricing, and marketing efforts. Create a detailed profile of your ideal client, including their industry, needs, and pain points. The more specific you are, the better you'll be able to attract and serve the right clients.

3. **Outline Your Services and Offerings:** What services do you offer, and how do they solve your clients' problems? Clearly define your core offerings, along with any additional services or packages. This section of your business plan should showcase the unique value you bring to the table and how your services meet the needs of your target market.

4. **Set Your Pricing Strategy:** Pricing can be one of the trickiest aspects of freelancing, but your business plan will help you tackle it with confidence. Research industry rates, consider your experience and expertise, and set pricing that reflects the value you provide. Don't forget to factor in your expenses, taxes, and desired income when setting your rates. This is also a good place to outline any discount policies or payment terms.

5. **Develop a Marketing Plan:** How will you attract clients and grow your business? Your marketing plan should include strategies for building your brand, networking, and promoting your services. Whether it's through social media, content marketing, or attending industry events, your marketing plan should outline how you'll reach your target market and stand out from the competition.

6. **Create a Financial Plan:** Your financial plan is the backbone of your business plan. It should include your income goals, projected expenses, and cash flow projections. This section helps you understand the financial health of your business and plan for future growth. It's also where you'll set your financial goals and outline strategies for achieving them, such as saving for taxes, building an emergency fund, or investing in your business.

7. **Set Milestones and Goals:** Break down your long-term vision into actionable milestones and goals. These could include income targets, client acquisition goals, or expanding your services. Setting specific, measurable goals will keep you motivated and focused, and give you a sense of accomplishment as you achieve

each milestone.

8. **Plan for Growth and Adaptation:** Freelancing is a dynamic field, and your business plan should reflect that. Include a section on growth strategies and how you plan to adapt to changes in the market. This could involve expanding your services, entering new markets, or investing in new skills and technologies. Being proactive about growth and adaptation will keep your business resilient and competitive.

Tips and Tricks for Creating a Business Plan that Works

Creating a business plan might sound daunting, but it doesn't have to be. Here are some tips and tricks to make the process smoother and more enjoyable:

Keep It Simple: Your business plan doesn't have to be a massive document. In fact, a one-page business plan can be incredibly effective. Focus on the essentials – your mission, market, services, pricing, and financial plan. The key is to create a document that's clear, concise, and easy to reference.

Use Templates and Tools: There are plenty of templates and tools available to help you create a business plan. Whether it's a simple Word document or a more structured business plan software, find a format that works for you. Templates can save you time and provide a helpful structure to follow.

Make It Your Own: Your business plan should reflect your unique personality and business style. Don't be afraid to add a personal touch, whether it's with your writing style, design, or the goals you set. This is your plan, so make sure it resonates with you and feels authentic.

Review and Revise Regularly: Your business plan isn't a static document – it's a living, breathing guide that should evolve with your business. Set aside time each quarter or year to review and revise your plan. Update your goals, adjust your strategies, and make sure your plan reflects the current state of your business.

Seek Feedback: Don't be afraid to ask for feedback on your business plan. Share it with a mentor, business coach, or trusted colleague. They can offer valuable insights and help you identify any gaps or areas for improvement.

Stay Inspired: Creating a business plan should be an inspiring process, not a chore. Take breaks, stay motivated, and remind yourself why you're doing this. Whether it's for financial independence, creative freedom, or building something you're passionate about, keep your "why" front and center.

Conclusion

Your business plan is more than just a document – it's a blueprint for your freelance success. With it, you'll have a clear vision, a solid foundation, and a practical guide to navigate the freelance world. Whether you're just starting out or looking to take your business to the next level, a well-crafted business plan will keep you on track, motivated, and ready to tackle whatever challenges come your way.

So, take the time to create your business plan, and watch as it transforms your freelance business from a series of day-to-day tasks into a thriving, sustainable enterprise. With your plan in hand, you'll be equipped to achieve your goals, adapt to changes, and build the freelance business of your dreams. Here's to your success, and the exciting journey ahead!

Chapter 3: Fueling Your Freedom: Crafting a Smart Budget for Your Freelance Business

***"D**on't tell me what you value, show me your budget, and I'll tell you what you value.* -Joe Biden

Budgeting Bliss

Freelancing is like sailing your own ship on the open sea. You have the freedom to chart your course, choose your destinations, and enjoy the breeze of independence. But with that freedom comes responsibility. And just like any good captain, you need a map – a financial blueprint – that guides your decisions and ensures you stay on course. That blueprint, my fellow freelancer, is your budget.

Budgeting might not sound as glamorous as landing a big client or launching a new project, but it's the unsung hero of your freelance business. It's the foundation that keeps your ship afloat, helps you weather financial storms, and sets you up for long-term success. In this chapter, we'll dive into why budgeting is crucial for freelancers and how you can create a budget that works for you. Get ready for a journey into the world of budgeting bliss!

Why Creating a Budget is Essential for Freelancers

So, why is budgeting such a big deal for freelancers? Let's explore the key reasons:

Stability in a Unpredictable World: As a freelancer, your income can be as unpredictable as the weather. One month, you're rolling in dough, and the next, you're scraping by. A budget helps smooth out these ups and downs by giving you a clear picture of your income and expenses. With a budget in place, you can plan for leaner months and avoid the stress of wondering how you'll pay the bills.

Empowerment and Control: Budgeting puts you in the driver's seat of your freelance business. Instead of feeling like your finances are controlling you, a budget gives you the power to make informed decisions. You know exactly where your money is going, what you can afford, and how much you need to save. It's like having a financial superpower that helps you navigate your business with confidence.

Achieving Your Goals: Whether you're saving for a dream vacation, investing in new equipment, or planning for retirement, a budget is your roadmap to achieving those goals. By setting aside money each month for your financial goals, you're taking intentional steps toward making them a reality. Without a budget, those goals remain just that – dreams that never quite materialize.

Preventing Debt: Debt is the iceberg that can sink your freelance ship. Without a budget, it's easy to overspend, rely on credit cards, or dip into savings when money is tight. A budget helps you live within your means, avoid unnecessary debt, and build a solid financial foundation. It's your best defense against the financial pitfalls that can derail your business.

Peace of Mind: Let's face it – freelancing can be stressful. But a budget brings peace of mind by providing clarity and structure to your finances. You know exactly where you stand financially, which reduces anxiety and helps you sleep better at night. It's like having a safety net that catches you when life gets unpredictable.

Practical Steps to Create a Budget That Works for You

Now that we've covered why budgeting is so important, let's dive into the practical steps to create a budget that works for your freelance business. Don't worry – Budgeting doesn't have to be boring or complicated. With the right approach, it can be a creative and empowering process.

Start with Your Income: The first step in creating a budget is to figure out your income. As a freelancer, your income might vary from month to month, so it's important to take an average. Look at your income over the past 6-12 months and calculate the average. This will give you a baseline to work with. If you're just starting out and don't have a lot of income data, make an educated guess based on your rates and projected work.

Track Your Expenses: Next, it's time to track your expenses. This includes both business and personal expenses. Start by listing out all your fixed expenses – things like rent, utilities, insurance, and subscriptions. Then, move on to variable expenses, such as groceries, entertainment, and business supplies. Don't forget to include irregular expenses like taxes, software renewals, and equipment purchases. Tracking your expenses gives you a clear picture of where your money is going and helps you identify areas where you can cut back if needed.

Categorize Your Expenses: Once you've tracked your expenses, it's helpful to categorize them. This allows you to see where you're spending the most and helps you allocate your income more effectively. Common categories for freelancers include rent/mortgage, utilities, groceries, transportation, business supplies, marketing, savings, taxes, and entertainment. You can create as many or as few categories as you like – just make sure they reflect your spending habits and priorities.

Set Financial Goals: Now that you have a clear picture of your income and expenses, it's time to set some financial goals. These could be short-term goals, like saving for a new laptop, or long-term goals, like building a retirement fund. Be specific about your goals and assign a dollar amount and timeline to each one. For example, "Save $1,000 for a new laptop in six months" or "Contribute $500 per month to my retirement account." Setting clear financial goals gives you something to work towards and helps you stay motivated.

Allocate Your Income: With your goals in mind, it's time to allocate your income to different categories. Start with your fixed expenses – these are non-negotiable and need to be covered first. Next, allocate money to your financial goals. Finally, divide the remaining income among your variable expenses, like groceries, entertainment, and business supplies. If your income is tight, you may need to adjust your spending or look for ways to increase your income. The key is to create a balance that allows you to cover your expenses, save for the future, and enjoy life along the way.

Using Budgeting Tools: There's no need to do all of this manually – budgeting tools can make the process much easier. Whether it's a simple spreadsheet or a dedicated budgeting app, find a tool that works for you. Budgeting apps like YNAB (You Need A Budget), Mint, or QuickBooks can help you track your income and expenses, set goals, and stay on top of your finances. The right tool can turn budgeting from a chore into a seamless part of your routine.

Review and Adjust Regularly: Your budget isn't set in stone – it's a living document that should evolve with your business. Set aside time each month to review your budget, track your progress, and make any necessary adjustments. Did you land a big project? Allocate some of that extra income to your savings or goals. Had a slow month? Cut back on non-essential spending. Regularly reviewing and adjusting your budget ensures that it stays relevant and helps you stay on track.

Tips and Tricks for Successful Budgeting

Now that you've got the basics down, here are some tips and tricks to take your budgeting game to the next level:

1. **Automate Your Savings:** One of the best ways to stick to your budget is to automate your savings. Set up automatic transfers from your checking account to your savings or retirement accounts. This way, you're paying yourself first and ensuring that your financial goals are funded before anything else.

2. **Keep Personal and Business Finances Separate:** It's tempting to mix personal and business finances, but it's a recipe for confusion. Keep them separate by using different accounts for personal and business expenses. This makes it easier to track your spending, manage taxes, and see how your business is performing.

3. **Plan for the Unexpected:** Life is full of surprises, and your budget should account for them. Build an emergency fund to cover unexpected expenses like medical bills, care repairs, or a sudden drop in income. Aim to save at least three to six months' worth of expenses – this cushion will give you peace of mind and help you weather any financial storms.

4. **Reward Yourself:** Budgeting doesn't have to be all work and no play. Build in small rewards for sticking to your budget or hitting your financial goals. It could be something as simple as treating yourself to a nice dinner or buying that book you've been eyeing. Rewards keep you motivated and make the budgeting process more enjoyable.

5. **Stay Flexible:** Your budget is a tool, not a strict set of rules. If something isn't working, don't be afraid to change it. Maybe you realize you're spending more on marketing than you anticipated, or you need to adjust your savings goals. Flexibility is key to making your budget work for you, so don't be afraid to tweak it as needed.

Conclusion

Budgeting might not be the most glamorous part of freelancing, but it's one of the most important. It's your financial blueprint, guiding your decisions, helping you achieve your goals, and keeping your business on track. With a budget in place, you'll feel empowered, in control, and ready to tackle whatever comes your way.

So, take the plunge and create a budget. Embrace the process, enjoy the clarity it brings, and watch as it transforms your freelance business from a day-to-day hustle into a well-oiled, financially secure operation. Here's to your budgeting bliss and the financial freedom that comes with it!

Chapter 4: The Art of Money Mapping: Tracking Your Income and Expenses

> "*A budget is telling your money where to go instead of wondering where it went.*" -Dave Ramsey

If freelancing is like being the captain of your own ship, then tracking your income and expenses is your compass. Without it, you're sailing blind, with no real sense of direction. Knowing where your money comes from and where it goes is crucial for keeping your freelance business afloat. Think of it as your personal treasure map, guiding you toward financial stability and success.

Now you might be asking, "Didn't we just discuss creating a budget? What's the difference between doing that and tracking income and expenses?" I'm glad you asked because sometimes the difference between these two tasks can confuse people. So let me explain.

Creating a budget and tracking income and expenses are two distinct but complementary financial tasks. **Creating a budget** is a *proactive step* where you plan and allocate your expected income toward various expenses, savings, and investments. It's like setting a financial roadmap for your business, determining how much money should be spent in different categories to meet your goals. On the other hand, **tracking income and expenses** is a *reactive task* that involves monitoring and recording your actual earnings and expenditures. This process helps you compare your real financial activity against your budget, ensuring you stay on course and make adjustments as needed. In essence, budgeting sets the plan, while tracking ensures you're following it.

In this chapter, we're going to dive into the art of money mapping – why tracking your income and expenses is non-negotiable, how to do it effectively, and a few playful tips and tricks to make the process a bit more fun. So, grab your compass, and let's start charting a course for financial clarity!

Why Tracking Your Income and Expenses is Crucial

First things first, why is it so important to keep a close eye on your income and expenses? Let's explore some key reasons:

Financial Clarity: Tracking your income and expenses gives you a clear picture of your financial situation. You'll know exactly how much money is coming in, where it's going, and what's left at the end of the day. Without this clarity, it's easy to overspend, miss out on tax deductions, or fall into the trap of thinking you have more money than you actually do.

Informed Decision-Making: When you have accurate financial data at your fingertips, you can make informed decisions about your business. Want to invest in new equipment? Thinking about raising your rates? Considering hiring help? All of these decisions are easier to make when you have a clear understanding of your income and expenses. It's like having a crystal ball that shows you the financial impact of your choices.

Tax Time Made Easy: Let's face it – taxes are a headache for most freelancers. But when you track your income and expenses throughout the year, tax time becomes a breeze. You'll have all the information you need to file your taxes accurately, claim deductions, and avoid any nasty surprises from the IRS. Plus, you'll be able to keep more of your hard-earned money in your pocket.

Budgeting and Goal-Setting: We talked about the importance of budgeting in the previous chapter, and tracking your income and expenses is a big part of that process. By knowing exactly how much you earn and spend, you can create a realistic budget and set achievable financial goals. Whether you're saving for a big purchase, planning for retirement, or just trying to build an emergency fund, tracking your finances is the first step toward reaching your goals.

Preventing Cash Flow Issues: Cash flow is the lifeblood of any freelance business. If you don't have enough cash coming in to cover your expenses, you're in trouble. By tracking your income and expenses, you can spot potential cash flow issues before they become a problem. You'll know when to tighten your belt when to chase down late payments, and when to ramp up your marketing efforts to bring in more business.

Peace of Mind: I've mentioned this one before and I'll probably mention it again before the end of the book because it's really important to any business person but especially for freelancers. There's something incredibly satisfying about knowing exactly where you stand financially. It reduces stress, helps you sleep better at night, and gives you the confidence to make bold moves in your business. Tracking your income and expenses is like having a safety net that catches you when things get shaky.

Practical Steps to Track Your Income and Expenses

Now that we've covered the why, let's get into the how. Tracking your income and expenses doesn't have to be a tedious chore. With the right approach, it can be a simple and even enjoyable part of running your freelance business.

Choose Your Tools: The first step is to choose the tools you'll use to track your income and expenses. There are plenty of options out there, from old-school pen and paper to sophisticated financial software. The key is to find something that works for you and stick with it. Popular tools include:

- **Spreadsheet Software:** Programs like Excel or Google Sheets are great for creating custom tracking sheets. You can set up columns for income, expenses, categories, and totals, and update them regularly.

- **Budgeting Apps:** Apps like QuickBooks, FreshBooks, or Wave are designed specifically for freelancers and small business owners. They allow you to track income and expenses, categorize transactions, and even generate reports.

- **Accounting Software:** If your business is more complex, accounting software like Xero or Sage might be the way to go. These tools offer more advanced features like invoicing, payroll, and tax preparation.

Track Every Penny: Once you've chosen your tools, it's time to start tracking. The key is to be consistent and track every penny that comes in and goes out. This means recording every payment you receive, every expense you incur, and every invoice you send. Don't forget to track irregular income and expenses, like one-off projects, refunds, or annual software renewals.

Categorize Your Transactions: To make sense of your financial data, it's important to categorize your transactions. This will help you see where your money is coming from and where it's going. Common categories for freelancers include:

- **Income:** Client payments, royalties, affiliate income, etc.

- **Expenses:** Rent, utilities, software, equipment, marketing, travel, etc.

- **Taxes:** Quarterly estimated tax payments, state and local taxes, etc.

- **Savings:** Emergency fund, retirement contributions, etc.

By categorizing your transactions, you'll be able to generate reports that show you how much you're earning, where you're spending the most, and how much you're saving.

Set Up a System: The best way to stay on top of your finances is to set up a system that works for you. This might mean setting aside time each week to update your tracking sheet, categorizing transactions as they happen, or using automation tools to do the work for you. The key is to find a routine that fits your schedule and stick with it.

Review Your Finances Regularly: Tracking your income and expenses is an ongoing process, not a one-time task. To get the most out of it, you need to review your finances regularly. This might mean checking your tracking sheet at the end of each month, generating reports every quarter, or doing a deep dive at the end of the year. Regular reviews will help you spot trends, identify areas where you can cut back, and make sure you're on track to meet your financial goals.

Adjust as Needed: Your income and expenses will fluctuate over time, so it's important to be flexible and adjust your tracking system as needed. If you notice that you're consistently overspending in a certain category, you might need to tighten your budget or look for ways to increase your income. If your business is growing and your expenses are becoming more complex, you might need to upgrade to more advanced tracking tools. The key is to stay on top of your finances and make adjustments as needed to keep your business on track.

Tips and Tricks for Effective Tracking

Tracking your income and expenses doesn't have to be a chore. With the right mindset and a few clever tricks, you can make it a seamless part of your freelance routine. Here are some tips to help you stay on top of your finances:

1. **Automate Where Possible:** Automation is your best friend when it comes to tracking income and expenses. Set up automatic bank feeds in your accounting software, schedule regular transfers to your savings account, and use apps that categorize transactions for you. The less manual work you have to do, the more likely you are to stay on top of your tracking.

2. **Keep Personal and Business Finances Separate:** I mentioned this in the previous chapter, but it's worth repeating – keep your personal and business finances separate. Use different bank accounts, credit cards, and tracking sheets for each. This will make it easier to see how your business is performing and avoid any confusion come tax time.

3. **Set Reminders:** It's easy to let tracking fall by the wayside when you're busy with client work, but consistency is key. Set reminders on your phone or calendar to update your tracking sheet, review your finances, and categorize transactions. A little nudge can go a long way in keeping you on track.

4. **Create a Financial Dashboard:** If you're a visual person, consider creating a financial dashboard that gives you a quick overview of your finances. This could be a simple spreadsheet with charts and graphs that show your income, expenses, and savings at a glance. A dashboard can make tracking more engaging and help you stay motivated.

5. **Celebrate Small Wins:** Tracking your income and expenses is hard work, so don't forget to celebrate your small wins along the way. Did you hit a sav-

ings goal? Treat yourself to something special. Did you manage to reduce your expenses? Give yourself a pat on the back. Celebrating your progress makes tracking more rewarding and helps you stay committed.

6. **Stay Curious:** Tracking your income and expenses is an opportunity to learn more about your business and your spending habits. Stay curious and look for patterns, trends, and areas for improvement. The more you understand your finances, the better equipped you'll be to make smart decisions and grow your business.

Conclusion

Tracking your income and expenses is like keeping a detailed map of your financial journey. It shows you where you've been, where you are, and where you're headed. With this map in hand, you can make informed decisions, avoid financial pitfalls, and navigate your freelance business with confidence.

So, embrace the art of money mapping and start tracking your income and expenses today. It might not be the most glamorous part of freelancing, but it's one of the most important. And with the right tools, a bit of consistency, and a dash of curiosity, you'll find that managing your finances becomes second nature. As you diligently chart your financial course, you'll gain the clarity, control, and peace of mind needed to steer your freelance business toward lasting success. Happy tracking!

Chapter 5: The Importance of Keeping Personal and Business Finances Separate

> *"A budget is more than just a series of numbers on a page; it is an embodiment of our values."* -Barack Obama

Imagine this: You're the rule of two distinct kingdoms – Personal Life and Freelance Business. Both kingdoms thrive under your reign, but they have different needs, different subjects, and different goals. Now, imagine if these two kingdoms were to merge, with no clear boundary separating them. Chaos, right? That's exactly what happens when you mix personal and business finances.

As a freelancer, keeping your personal and business finances separate isn't just a good practice – it's essential for the health of both your business and your personal life. This chapter will delve into why this separation is crucial, provide actionable steps to make it happen, and offer some tips and tricks to keep things running smoothly. So, let's embark on this journey to financial clarity and freedom!

Why Separating Personal and Business Finances is Crucial

Before we get into the how, let's talk about the why. Why should you bother keeping your personal and business finances separate? Here are some compelling reasons:

Clear Financial Picture: When you keep your finances separate, you can clearly see how your freelance business is performing. You'll know exactly how much money your business is making, where it's being spent, and whether you're turning a profit. Without this separation, your financial picture becomes muddled, making it difficult to assess your business's health.

Simplified Tax Preparation: Tax time can be stressful, but separating your finances makes it much easier. When personal and business expenses are mixed together, sorting through receipts and statements becomes a nightmare. Keeping them separate allows you to easily identify deductible business expenses, prepare accurate tax returns, and avoid costly mistakes or audits.

Professionalism and Credibility: Having separate finances for your business enhances your professionalism and credibility. Clients, vendors, and even potential lenders will take you more seriously when you manage your business finances independently from your personal ones. It shows that you're running a legitimate business, not just a side hustle.

Legal Protection: If you operate as a limited liability company (LLC) or another legal entity, separating your finances is crucial for maintaining your limited liability status. Mixing personal and business finances can "pierce the corporate veil," exposing your personal assets to potential legal claims against your business. Keeping your finances separate helps protect your personal assets from business liabilities.

Better Budgeting and Planning: When your personal and business finances are intertwined, it's difficult to create accurate budgets and financial plans. Separating them allows you to create targeted budgets for your business and personal life, helping you allocate resources more effectively and achieve your financial goals.

Peace of Mind: I know I keep mentioning this one but it's definitely so important for freelancers. Separating your finances gives you peace of mind. You'll know exactly where your money is going, how your business is performing, and whether you're on track to meet your financial goals. This clarity reduces stress, helps you make informed decisions, and keeps you in control of your financial destiny.

Action Steps to Separate Personal and Business Finances

Now that we've established why separating your finances is important, let's get into the nitty-gritty of how to do it. Here are some practical steps to help you draw a clear line between your personal and business finances:

Open Separate Bank Accounts: The first and most important step is to open separate bank accounts for your personal and business finances. Use your business account for all business-related income and expenses, and your personal account for everything else. This simple step creates a clear boundary between your two financial worlds.

Get a Business Credit Card: Along with a separate bank account, consider getting a business credit card. Use this card exclusively for business expenses – whether it's buying office supplies, paying for software subscriptions, or covering travel costs. This not only keeps your finances separate but also helps you build business credit, which can be valuable if you ever need to secure financing.

Set Up an Accounting System: Implementing an accounting system is key to keeping your finances organized. Whether you use accounting software like QuickBooks or a simple spreadsheet, make sure to track all your business income and expenses separately from your personal finances. Regularly update your records to stay on top of your cash flow and financial position.

Pay Yourself a Salary: One of the best ways to keep your finances separate is to pay yourself a regular salary from your business account to your personal account. This creates a clear distinction between your business earnings and personal income. Plus, it helps you budget for personal expenses more effectively.

Create a Business Budget: Just like you would for your personal finances, create a budget for your business. Outline your expected income, necessary expenses, and allocate funds for savings, taxes, and investments. A business budget ensures that you're not dipping into personal funds to cover business expenses and vice versa.

Separate Record-Keeping: Maintain separate records for your personal and business finances. Keep all business-related receipts, invoices, and statements organized and easily accessible. This will make it easier to track expenses, prepare for tax season, and manage your finances effectively.

Consult with a Professional: If you're unsure about how to separate your finances or manage your business accounting, consider consulting with a financial advisor or accountant. They can help you set up the right systems, ensure compliance with tax laws, and offer advice on managing your finances effectively.

Tips and Tricks for Maintaining Separate Finances

Separating your finances is one thing, but maintaining that separation can be a challenge, especially when life gets busy. Here are some tips and tricks to help you stay on track:

1. **Use Automation:** Take advantage of automation tools to keep your finances organized. Set up automatic transfers from your business account to your personal account for your salary, automate bill payments for business expenses, and use accounting software that automatically categorizes transactions. Automation reduces the chances of mixing personal and business finances.

2. **Avoid Personal Spending on Business Accounts:** It can be tempting to use your business account or credit card for personal expenses, especially when you're in a pinch. But resist the urge! Keep personal spending separate to avoid confusion and potential tax issues. If you accidentally use your business account for a personal expense, make a note of it and reimburse your business from your personal funds.

3. **Review Your Finances Regularly:** Schedule regular check-ins with yourself to review your finances. This could be a weekly, monthly, or quarterly task, depending on your business's complexity. During these check-ins, make sure your business and personal accounts are balanced, review your budgets, and adjust as needed. Regular reviews help you catch any mistakes early and keep you on track.

4. **Use a Personal Finance App:** Consider Using a personal finance app like Mint or YNAB to manage your personal finances, while keeping your business finances separate in a dedicated accounting software. These apps can help you

budget, track spending, and manage personal savings without mixing them with business finances.

5. **Create a System for Reimbursements:** If you ever need to use personal funds for business expenses or vice versa, create a system for tracking and reimbursing those expenses. For example, if you use your personal credit card to pay for a business expense, transfer the exact amount from your business account to your personal account as soon as possible and record the transaction.

6. **Educate Yourself:** Take the time to educate yourself about business finance management. The more you know about accounting, taxes, and financial planning, the easier it will be to keep your finances separate and manage them effectively. Consider taking a course, reading books, or attending workshops on the topic.

7. **Celebrate Milestones Separately:** When your business hits a financial milestone, celebrate it with your business finances! For example, if your business reaches a revenue goal, reinvest some of the profits into the business, like upgrading equipment or taking a course to enhance your skills. Keep personal milestones and celebrations separate to reinforce the divide between your two financial worlds.

Conclusion: Embrace the Separation

Keeping your personal and business finances separate might feel like an extra hassle at first, but it's one of the smartest moves you can make as a freelancer. This separation not only gives you a clear view of your business's financial health but also simplifies tax preparation, enhances your professionalism, and protects your personal assets. By implementing the action steps and tips in this chapter, you'll set yourself up for financial success and peace of mind.

Remember, you're the ruler of two kingdoms, and each one deserves its own treasury. Embrace the separation, and you'll find that both your personal life and your freelance business will thrive in their own right. Keep those boundaries clear, and you'll be well on your way to a prosperous and stress-free freelance journey!

Chapter 6: Setting Clear Payment Terms

> *"If you do not know how to care for money, money will stay away from you."* -Robert Kiyosaki

Welcome to the wild, wild west of freelancing, where you're the sheriff, judge, and jury when it comes to getting paid. In the land of freelancing, there's one golden rule that separates the successful from the struggling: **Set clear payment terms.**

Imagine going on a road trip without a map. You'd probably end up lost, frustrated, and out of gas somewhere in the middle of nowhere. That's exactly what freelancing without clear payment terms is like. It's a journey with no direction, and trust me, you don't want to get stuck in a ghost town where your payments disappear into thin air.

In this chapter, we're going to dive into why setting clear payment terms is absolutely essential for your freelance business, what those terms should or could be, and how to make sure everyone's playing by the same rules. We'll finish up with some action steps and tips to help you master the art of payment terms. Ready to take the reins? Let's ride!

Why Setting Clear Payment Terms is Crucial

First things first, let's talk about why setting clear payment terms is so important. After all, you're not just a freelancer – you're a business owner. And every good business owner knows that cash flow is the lifeblood of their business. Without clear payment terms, you're leaving your financial well-being up to chance. Here's why that's a big no-no:

Cash Flow Management: Clear payment terms help you manage your cash flow effectively. When you know exactly when you'll get paid, you can plan your finances accordingly. This ensures you have enough cash on hand to cover your expenses, pay yourself, and reinvest in your business.

Avoiding Payment Delays: If you don't set clear payment terms upfront, clients may take their sweet time paying you – or worse, forget to pay you altogether. By setting expectations from the start, you reduce the risk of late payments and the stress that comes with chasing down money you're owed.

Professionalism and Boundaries: Setting payment terms shows that you're a professional who takes your work seriously. It establishes clear boundaries between you and your clients, letting them know that while you're here to deliver great work, you also expect to be compensated fairly and on time.

Minimizing Misunderstandings: Clear payment terms help avoid misunderstandings and disputes. When both you and your client know exactly what's expected, there's less room for confusion. This leads to smoother working relationships and a better experience for both parties.

Legal Protection: If a client fails to pay you, clear payment terms give you a solid foundation to stand on if you need to take legal action. Terms outlined in a contract or agreement can be enforced, giving you the legal backing you need to protect your business.

Building Trust: Setting payment terms early in the relationship builds trust between you and your clients. It shows that you're transparent about your expectations and that you're committed to a fair and straightforward working relationship.

What Payment Terms Should

Be

Include

d

Now that we've established the why, let's move on to the what. What exactly should your payment terms include? Here are some key components to consider when crafting your terms:

Payment Amount: This is the most obvious, but it's worth stating – your payment terms should clearly outline how much the client will pay you for your services. Whether it's a flat fee, hourly rate, or per-project charge, make sure the amount is agreed upon and documented.

Payment Schedule: Determine when you'll be paid and include this in your terms. Will you require a deposit upfront, with the remainder due upon completion? Will you be paid in milestones, with installments after certain phases of the project are completed? Or will you invoice monthly? Set clear expectations so there's no ambiguity.

Payment Methods: Specify how you want to be paid. Do you accept bank transfers, PayPal, credit cards, or other payment methods? Include this in your terms so your client knows how to send payment and you can avoid delays due to confusion over payment methods.

Late Fees: To encourage prompt payment, consider including a late fee clause in your terms. State that payments not received by the due date will incur a late fee (e.g. 1.5% of the invoice amount per month.) This can be a powerful motivator for clients to pay on time.

Project Scope and Revisions: Include details about what's included in the project scope and how many revisions are allowed before additional fees apply. This prevents clients from endlessly requesting changes and ensures you're fairly compensated for any extra work.

Kill Fee: A kill fee is a predetermined amount that the client agrees to pay if the project is canceled after you've already begun working. This protects you from losing out on income if the client decides to pull the plug halfway through the project.

Payment Terms Length: Specify how many days the client has to pay your invoice once it's been issued. Common terms include Net 30 (payment due within 30 days of the invoice date), Net 15, or even immediate payment upon receipt.

Consequences for Non-Payment: Outline the steps you'll take if the client fails to pay. This could include ceasing work until payment is received, sending the debt to collections, or taking legal action. While it's rare to have to enforce these terms, having them in place is a safety net.

Action Steps for Implementing Clear Payment Terms

Setting clear payment terms is one thing, but how do you go about implementing them? Here are some actionable steps to help you get started:

Create a Standard Contract: Develop a standard contract template that includes your payment terms. This contract should be used for every client, with any necessary adjustments made based on the specifics of each project. A contract solidifies your terms in writing and protects both you and the client.

Discuss Terms Upfront: Don't wait until the end of the project to discuss payment. Talk about your payment terms during the initial negotiation phase with your client. Make sure they understand and agree to the terms before any work begins. This sets clear expectations and avoids surprises later on.

Get a Deposit: One of the best ways to protect yourself is to require a deposit before starting work. A deposit not only secures your payment but also shows the client's commitment to the project. Common deposit amounts range from 25% to 50% of the total project fee.

Invoice Promptly: Once the work is completed or a payment milestone is reached, send your invoice immediately. Don't delay, as prompt invoicing reinforces the importance of timely payment. Include all relevant details on the invoice, such as the due date, payment methods, and any late fees.

Follow Up on Late Payments: If a client misses a payment deadline, don't hesitate to follow up. A polite reminder email is usually enough to prompt payment. If payment is still not received, refer to your contract's late fee and non-payment clauses and take appropriate action.

Review and Update Terms Regularly: As your business grows and evolves, your payment terms may need to be adjusted. Review your terms regularly and make updates as needed. For example, you might decide to shorten payment terms from Net 30 to Net 15 if you find clients are consistently paying late.

Tips and Tricks for Mastering Payment Terms

Now that you've got the basics down, here are some tips and tricks to help you fine-tune your payment terms and ensure you get paid on time, every time:

1. **Be Transparent and Fair:** When setting payment terms, aim for transparency and fairness. Clients are more likely to agree to terms that are clearly explained and reasonable. If you're too rigid or demanding, you might scare off potential clients. Strike a balance that protects your interests while being fair to the client.

2. **Use Invoicing Software:** Invest in invoicing software that automates the billing process. Tools like FreshBooks, QuickBooks, or Wave allow you to create professional invoices, set payment terms, and even automate follow-up reminders for late payments. Automation saves time and reduces the risk of human error.

3. **Be Flexible with Payment Methods:** While it's important to specify your preferred payment methods, being flexible can help you get paid faster. If a client prefers to pay via a method you don't normally accept, consider accommodating them if it means quicker payment.

4. **Maintain a Positive Relationship:** Building and maintaining a positive relationship with your clients can go a long way in ensuring timely payment. When clients value your work and enjoy working with you, they're more likely to respect your payment terms. Communication and professionalism are key.

5. **Consider Offering Discounts for Early Payment:** To incentivize clients to pay early, consider offering a small discount for payments received before the due date. For example, you could offer a 2% discount for payments made within

10 days on a Net 30 invoice. While it might reduce your earnings slightly, it can improve your cash flow.

6. **Always Be Prepared to Walk Away:** If a client refuses to agree to your payment terms or consistently pays late, it may be time to walk away. Protecting your financial well-being is more important than keeping a client who doesn't respect your business. Stand firm in your terms and prioritize working with clients who value your services.

Conclusion: Make Payment Terms Your Superpower

Setting clear payment terms is like putting on your financial superhero cape. It empowers you to take control of your freelance business, protect your cash flow, and ensure you're paid fairly and on time. By following the steps outlined in this chapter, you'll not only safeguard your income but also build stronger, more professional relationships with your clients.

Remember, You're not just a freelancer – you're the boss of your own business. And every great boss knows the importance of setting the rules of the game. So, saddle up, set those payment terms, and ride confidently into the sunset of freelance success!

Chapter 7: The Art of the Invoice

> *"The key factor that will determine your financial future is not the economy; the key factor is your philosophy."* -Jim Rohn

Freelance is a dance, and like any good dance, timing is everything. But instead of waltzing around a ballroom, we're talking about the dance of money – specifically, the importance of invoicing promptly and following up. If you've ever found yourself anxiously waiting for a payment to hit your account, wondering if your invoice somehow got lost in the digital ether, this chapter is for you.

Let's face it: freelancing is fantastic, but it comes with its own set of challenges. Chief among them is the fact that you're not on a payroll. No bi-weekly direct deposits here! Instead, you're responsible for making sure that money comes in – and that starts with a humble invoice. It might not be the most glamorous part of your business, but it's absolutely one of the most important. So, let's dive into why prompt invoicing and diligent follow-up can make or break your freelance business, and how you can master this art like a pro.

Why Prompt Invoicing is Crucial

When you finish a project, it can be tempting to take a deep breath, pat yourself on the back, and move on to the next task. But hold up! There's one more step before you wrap up: invoicing. Here's why getting that invoice out promptly is essential:

Cash Flow is King: You've probably heard the phrase "cash flow is king" more times than you can count, but it's true. Without a steady stream of income, even the most talented freelancer can find themselves in hot water. Prompt invoicing ensures that your cash flow remains consistent, allowing you to pay your bills, invest in your business, and keep the lights on.

Sets the Tone for Professionalism: Sending an invoice quickly after completing a project signals to your client that you're on top of your game. It shows that you're organized, reliable, and serious about your work. This can lead to a stronger, more trusting relationship with your clients.

Reduces the Risk of Forgetfulness: Both you and your client are busy people, and it's easy for things to slip through the cracks. The longer you wait to invoice, the more likely it is that your client will forget about the project, making it easier for your payment to be delayed – or forgotten altogether.

Increases the Likelihood of Prompt Payment: Clients are more likely to pay quickly if they receive the invoice while the project is still fresh in their minds. It's a psychological thing – when they've just received your fantastic work, they're more inclined to settle up right away.

Avoids Financial Bottlenecks: Delayed invoicing can lead to a pile-up of pending payments, which can create a financial bottleneck. You don't want to be in a situation where multiple invoices are out, but none are being paid because you didn't send them out in a timely manner.

The Follow-Up Dance

So, you've sent your invoice – great! But what happens if the payment doesn't show up in your account by the due date? Enter the follow-up dance. This step is just as crucial as sending the invoice itself, and here's why:

Ensures You Get Paid: The most obvious reason to follow up is to make sure you get paid. Sometimes clients simply need a gentle reminder, and following up increases the chances that they'll take action.

Maintains Healthy Cash Flow: Following up on unpaid invoices helps maintain the steady cash flow that's so critical for your business. It's all about keeping that money coming in on a regular basis so you're never caught short.

Reinforces Professional Boundaries: When you follow up on an unpaid invoice, you're reminding your client that this is a business transaction and that you expect to be paid for your work. It reinforces the boundaries of your professional relationship and shows that you take your business seriously.

Prevents Financial Strain: Unpaid invoices can lead to financial strain, especially if you're relying on that money to cover your expenses. By following up, you're actively working to prevent financial stress and keep your business running smoothly.

Builds Accountability: Following up shows your clients that you're accountable and expect the same from them. It encourages a sense of responsibility and can lead to a more respectful and cooperative working relationship.

Action Steps for Prompt Invoicing and Effective Follow-Up

Now that we've covered the why, let's talk about the how. Here are some actionable steps to help you master the art of prompt invoicing and effective follow-up:

Create an Invoicing Schedule: Set aside specific times in your week to handle invoicing. Whether it's at the end of each project or once a week, having a dedicated time ensures that invoicing doesn't slip through the cracks.

Use Invoicing Software: Invest in invoicing software like FreshBooks, QuickBooks, or Wave. These tools make it easy to create professional invoices, set due dates, and even automate reminders for late payments. They can also track your invoices and alert you when it's time to follow up.

Send Invoices Immediately: Make it a habit to send your invoice as soon as the project is completed. The quicker you send it, the quicker you'll get paid. If you're waiting for feedback or approval before finalizing the invoice, send it as soon as you get the green light.

Set Clear Payment Terms: Your invoice should clearly state the payment terms, including the due date, accepted payment methods, and any late fees. This sets the expectation from the start and gives you a solid basis for following up if the payment is late.

Follow Up Promptly: If the payment isn't received by the due date, don't wait – follow up immediately. Send a polite reminder email that references the invoice number, the amount due, and the original due date. A simple, friendly nudge is often all that's needed to get the payment process moving.

Stay Persistent but Professional: If the first follow-up doesn't result in payment, continue to follow up regularly. Stay persistent, but always remain professional and polite. Your goal is to get paid, not to alienate your client.

Keep Communication Open: Sometimes there's a legitimate reason for a delayed payment, like a client's cash flow issues or an internal processing delay. Keep the lines of communication open, and be willing to work with your client if they need a bit more time – just make sure you're compensated for your patience.

Document Everything: Keep records of all your invoices, follow-up emails, and any communication related to payment. This documentation can be invaluable if you ever need to escalate the issue or take legal action.

Tips and Tricks for Invoicing and Following Up Like a Pro

To wrap things up, here are some tips and tricks to help you fine-tune your invoicing and follow-up process:

1. **Personalize Your Invoices:** Add a personal touch to your invoices by including your logo, branding, and a thank-you note. This not only makes your invoice look professional but also leaves a positive impression on your client.

2. **Offer Multiple Payment Options:** Make it as easy as possible for your clients to pay you by offering multiple payment options. This could include bank transfers, credit cards, PayPal, or even cryptocurrency if you're so inclined. The easier it is for them to pay, the quicker you'll get paid.

3. **Use Incentives:** Consider offering a small discount for early payments. For

example, you could offer a 2% discount if the invoice is paid within 10 days. This can motivate clients to pay quickly, improving your cash flow.

4. **Be Clear and Concise:** Make sure your invoice is easy to read and understand. Include all the necessary details, such as the invoice number, date, due date, amount due, and a description of the work completed. The clearer your invoice, the less likely there will be delays due to confusion.

5. **Automate Your Reminders:** If you're using invoicing software, take advantage of automated reminders. Set up reminders to be sent a few days before the due date and again if the payment is late. Automation saves you time and ensures that you don't forget to follow up.

6. **Charge Late Fees:** If a client consistently pays late, consider implementing a late fee. This can serve as a deterrent for future late payments and ensure that you're compensated for the inconvenience.

7. **Know When to Escalate:** If you've followed up multiple times and still haven't received payment, it may be time to escalate the situation. This could involve hiring a collection agency, pursuing legal action, or cutting ties with the client. While these are last-resort options, it's important to know when to take them.

Conclusion: Master the Dance of Invoicing

Invoicing and following up might not be the most exciting part of freelancing, but they are absolutely essential. By mastering the art of prompt invoicing and diligent follow-up, you'll ensure that your cash flow remains steady, your business stays healthy, and you're compensated fairly for your hard work.

Remember, freelancing is a dance, and you're the one leading. So, take charge, set the tempo, and don't be afraid to nudge your partners – your clients – into keeping up with the rhythm. After all, getting paid isn't just a goal; it's a necessity. So, get out there, invoice promptly, follow up like a pro, and keep your freelance business grooving to the beat of success!

Chapter 8: Don't Put All Your Eggs in One Basket

> *"In my opinion, the most significant benefit of a diversified portfolio is psychological stability when you need it the most."* -Naved Abdali

Imagine you're standing in the middle of a beautiful garden. In one corner, there's a single, massive tree, towering over everything else. It's impressive, sure, but what happens if a storm hits and that tree falls? Your garden would look pretty bare, right? Now, picture a garden filled with a variety of plants – tall trees, colorful flowers, sturdy shrubs. If one plant withers, the others still thrive, keeping the garden lush and vibrant.

That garden is your freelance business, and each plant represents a different income stream. Diversifying your income streams is like planting multiple seeds in your garden – some may bloom more than others, but together they create a thriving, resilient ecosystem. In this chapter, we're going to explore why diversifying your income streams is crucial for your freelance success, how to go about it, and share some action steps, tips, and tricks to get you started.

Why Diversifying Your Income Streams is Crucial

As a freelancer, you've probably heard the saying, "Don't put all your eggs in one basket." It's sage advice, especially when it comes to your income. Here's why diversifying your income streams is so important:

Stability and Security: Freelancing can be a rollercoaster ride. One month, you're swimming in projects, and the next, you're staring at an empty inbox. By diversifying your income streams, you create a safety net that cushions the blow when one income source dries up. If a client stops sending work your way or a project falls through, you've got other sources to keep the cash flowing.

Flexibility and Freedom: Having multiple income streams gives you the freedom to pick and choose the work that excites you the most. It also means you're not beholden to any single client or project, allowing you to take risks, experiment with new ideas, and grow your business in different directions.

Growth and Expansion: Diversifying your income streams is a key driver of business growth. When you rely on just one or two sources of income, your growth is limited by the capacity of those streams. But when you diversify, you open up new opportunities for earning more and scaling your business.

Financial Independence: One of the biggest perks of freelancing is the potential for financial independence. By diversifying your income streams, you're taking control of your financial future. You're not just surviving – you're thriving, building a business that supports your goals and dreams.

Resilience to Market Changes: The freelance landscape is always changing. Trends come and go, industries evolve, and economic conditions fluctuate. Diversifying your income streams makes your business more resilient to these changes, ensuring you can adapt and continue to succeed no matter what happens.

Ways to Diversify Your Income Streams

Now that we've covered why diversifying your income is so important, let's talk about how to do it. Here are some tried-and-true ways to create multiple income streams as a freelancer:

Offer a Range of Services: If you're a writer, why not add editing or content strategy to your repertoire? If you're a designer, consider offering branding consultations or creating templates for sale. By broadening your service offerings, you can attract a wider range of clients and increase your earning potential.

Create Digital Products: Digital products are a fantastic way to generate passive income. Think eBooks, online courses, design templates, or stock photos. Once you create these products, they can continue to generate income with little ongoing effort. Plus, they allow you to share your expertise with a broader audience.

Start a Blog or YouTube Channel: Content creation is a great way to diversify your income. A blog or YouTube channel can bring in revenue through ads, sponsored content, affiliate marketing, or selling your own products and services. It's also a good way to build your personal brand and showcase your expertise.

Offer Coaching or Consulting: If you've got experience under your belt, why not share it with others? Offering coaching or consulting services can be a lucrative addition to your income streams. Whether it's one-on-one sessions, group coaching, or consulting on specific projects, there are plenty of ways to turn your knowledge into income.

Affiliate Marketing: Affiliate marketing involves promoting other people's products or services and earning a commission on any sales made through your referral. It's a relatively low-effort way to generate additional income, especially if you already have a blog, social media following, or email list.

Freelance on Different Platforms: If you usually find clients through one platform, consider expanding to others. For example, if you're on Upwork, try offering your services on Fiverr or LinkedIn ProFinder as well. Each platform has a different audience (I talk in detail about that in my book, From Likes to Profits), and by tapping into multiple markets, you increase your chances of finding new clients.

Teaching and Workshops: Share your skills by teaching classes or workshops, either in person or online. Platforms like Skillshare, Udemy, and Teachable make it easy to create and sell courses. Teaching not only diversifies your income but also positions you as an expert in your field.

Sell Physical Products: If your work has a visual or tactile element, consider selling physical products. For example, if you're a designer, you could sell prints or merchandise featuring your designs. If you're a writer, you could sell signed copies of your books or custom journals.

Action Steps to Get Started

Ready to diversify your income streams? Here are some action steps to help you get started:

Identify Your Strengths and Interests: Start by taking stock of your skills, strengths, and interests. What do you enjoy doing? What are you good at? This will help you identify potential income streams that align with your passions and expertise.

Research the Market: Once you have some ideas, research the market to see what's already out there. Look at what other freelancers in your field are offering, and identify gaps or opportunities where you can stand out.

Start Small and Test the Waters: You don't have to launch all your new income streams at once. Start small and test the waters. For example, if you're interested in creating digital products, start with a simple eBook or template. If it does well, you can expand into more products.

Set Clear Goals: As with any business venture, it's important to set clear goals for your new income streams. How much do you want to earn? How much time are you willing to invest? Setting goals will help you stay focused and measure your progress.

Create a Plan: Once you've identified your new income streams and set goals, create a plan for how you'll implement them. This might include setting up a website, creating marketing materials, or scheduling time to work on your new projects.

Monitor and Adjust: As you start to diversify your income, keep track of what's working and what's not. Be prepared to adjust your strategy based on your results. Some income streams may take off quickly, while others might need more time to gain traction.

Tips and Tricks for Successful Diversification

Here are some tips and tricks to help you successfully diversify your income streams:

1. **Focus on Quality, Not Quantity:** It's better to have a few well-developed income streams than to spread yourself too thin with too many. Focus on quality over quantity – make sure each income stream is sustainable and aligns with your

overall business goals.

2. **Leverage Your Existing Clients:** Your existing clients can be a great source of new income. If you're adding new services or products, let your current clients know – they might be interested in what you have to offer, or they might refer you to others.

3. **Build Passive Income Streams:** Passive income is the holy grail of diversification. Look for opportunities to create income streams that require minimal ongoing effort, like digital products, affiliate marketing, or ad revenue from a blog or YouTube channel.

4. **Network and Collaborate:** Don't be afraid to reach out to other freelancers or businesses for collaboration opportunities. Joint ventures, partnerships, and collaborations can open up new income streams that you might not have access to on your own.

5. **Keep Learning:** The more you know, the more opportunities you'll have to diversify your income. Stay curious and keep learning – whether it's taking a course, attending a workshop, or simply experimenting with new ideas.

6. **Be Patient:** Diversifying your income streams takes time. Be patient and give yourself the space to experiment and grow. Not every income stream will be an immediate success, but with persistence and effort, you'll build a solid foundation for long-term financial success.

Conclusion: Diversify and Thrive

Diversifying your income streams is like planting a variety of seeds in your freelance garden. Some will grow quickly, others may take time to bloom, but together they'll create a vibrant, thriving business that's resilient, flexible, and full of potential.

By taking the time to diversify your income, you're not just protecting yourself from the ups and downs of freelancing – you're creating a business that supports your goals, fuels your passion, and gives you the freedom to live life on your terms. So, go ahead and plant those seeds – your freelance garden is about to flourish like never before!

Chapter 9: Saving for Taxes

> *"A fine is a tax for doing something wrong. A tax is a fine for doing something right."* -Anonymous

Imagine this: you're walking down a sunny street with a skip in your step. Your freelance business is booming, clients are happy, and you're feeling on top of the world. But then, out of nowhere, a cloud looms overhead. It's not rain – it's the tax man. Yikes! Suddenly, that carefree stroll turns into a frantic dash to scrape together enough cash to pay Uncle Sam (or whoever it is in your country that you pay taxes to.) Not exactly the happy ending you were hoping for, right?

Now, imagine a different scenario. You're still strutting down that sunny street, but this time, you've got a secret weapon – a stash of cash set aside just for taxes. When the tax man comes knocking, you calmly reach into your financial toolkit, hand over the payment, and continue on your merry way. No stress, no panic, just smooth sailing.

That's the power of saving for taxes. It's not the most fun or glamorous part of freelancing, but it's one of the critical parts of your business. In this chapter, we're going to dive into why saving for taxes is essential, how to determine how much you need to save, and give you some action steps, tips, and tricks to make tax season a breeze.

Why Saving for Taxes is a Must

Let's be real – taxes are no one's favorite subject. But as a freelancer, they're a part of life, and ignoring them is not an option. Here's why saving for taxes is so important:

Avoiding a Financial Crisis: The last thing you want is to be caught off guard when tax season rolls around. If you haven't saved enough, you could find yourself scrambling to come up with the cash, which could lead to borrowing, selling assets, or even worse, not being able to pay at all. By saving for taxes throughout the year, you avoid the stress and potential financial crisis that comes with being unprepared.

Maintaining Cash Flow: Taxes can be a big hit to your cash flow if you haven't planned for them. By setting aside money for taxes regularly, you ensure that your cash flow remains steady. You won't have to dip into your emergency fund, delay paying bills, or miss out on opportunities because of a surprise tax bill.

Peace of Mind: Knowing that you have enough saved to cover your taxes gives you peace of mind. You can focus on your work, your clients, and growing your business without the constant worry of an impending tax bill hanging over your head. It's like having a financial safety net that lets you sleep soundly at night.

Building Good Financial Habits: Saving for taxes is part of building strong financial habits that will serve you well throughout your freelance career. It teaches you discipline, foresight, and the importance of planning ahead – all essential skills for managing your freelance business successfully.

Compliance with the Law: Let's not forget the most obvious reason – paying your taxes is a legal obligation. Failing to pay can result in penalties, interest charges, and even legal action. By saving for taxes, you're ensuring that you meet your legal obligations and avoid any unwanted trouble with the IRS.

How to Determine How Much to Save

Okay, so saving for taxes is important – but how much do you actually need to save? Here's a step-by-step guide to help you figure it out:

Estimate Your Income: The first step is to estimate your annual income. This might be tricky if your freelance income fluctuates, but you can use your previous year's income as a starting point. If you're just starting out, make an educated guess based on your rates and expected workload.

Know Your Tax Rate: Next, you'll need to know your tax rate. As a freelancer, you're responsible for both income tax and self-employment tax (which covers Social Security and Medicare). Your tax rate will depend on your income level, so it's a good idea to check the IRS tax brackets or consult a tax professional.

Calculate Your Tax Obligation: Once you have your estimated income and tax rate, you can calculate your tax obligation. Multiply your estimated income by your tax rate to get a rough idea of how much you'll own in taxes. Don't forget to include both federal and state taxes, if applicable.

Factor in Deductions and Credits: Freelancers are eligible for a variety of tax deductions and credits that can lower your tax bill. These might include business expenses, home office deductions, retirement contributions, and more. Be sure to factor these into your calculations to get a more accurate estimate of your tax obligation.

Set Aside a Percentage of Your Income: Based on your calculations, determine what percentage of your income you need to set aside for taxes. A good rule of thumb is to save 25% to 30% of your income for taxes, but this can vary depending on your specific situation. It's better to save a little more than you think you'll need than to come up short.

Adjust Throughout the Year: As you earn more or less than expected, adjust your savings accordingly. If you have a particularly good month, save a little extra. If business is slow, you might need to tighten your belt a bit. The key is to stay on top of your income and adjust your savings as needed.

Action Steps to Get Started

Ready to start saving for taxes? Here are some action steps to help you get started:

Open a Separate Savings Account: One of the easiest ways to save for taxes is to open a separate savings account specifically for your tax savings. This keeps your tax money separate from your regular funds and reduces the temptation to dip into it for other expenses.

Automate Your Savings: If you struggle with remembering to save, automate the process. Set up automatic transfers from your business account to your tax savings account each time you get paid. This way, the money is saved before you even have a chance to spend it.

Track Your Income and Expenses: Keeping accurate records of your income and expenses is crucial for determining how much you need to save for taxes. Use accounting software or a simple spreadsheet to track your earnings and deductions throughout the year. This will make it easier to estimate your tax obligation and ensure you're saving enough.

Make Quarterly Estimated Payments: As a freelancer, you're required to make quarterly estimated tax payments to the IRS. This helps you avoid a large tax bill at the end of the year and any associated penalties. Use your tax savings to make these payments on time and keep track of your payment schedule.

Consult a Tax Professional: If you're unsure about how much to save or need help with your taxes, consider consulting a tax professional. They can provide personalized advice based on your income, deductions, and tax situation, ensuring you're saving the right amount and taking advantage of all available tax benefits.

Tips and Tricks for Stress-Free Tax Saving

Saving for taxes doesn't have to be a daunting task. Here are some tips and tricks to make it easier:

1. **Save Windfalls and Extra Income:** If you receive unexpected income, such as a bonus or a large project payment, consider saving a portion of it for taxes. This can help you build up your tax savings more quickly and reduce the burden of saving from your regular income.

2. **Review Your Savings Regularly:** Periodically review your tax savings to ensure you're on track. If you're falling behind, take steps to catch up, such as cutting back on expenses or setting aside a higher percentage of your income. Regular reviews will help you stay proactive and avoid any surprises come tax season.

3. **Stay Organized:** Keep all your tax-related documents organized throughout the year. This includes receipts, invoices, and records of your estimated tax

payments. Being organized will make it easier to file your taxes and ensure you're claiming all the deductions and credits you're entitled to.

4. **Celebrate Small Wins:** Saving for taxes can feel like a chore, so celebrate your progress along the way. Whether it's reaching a savings milestone or making a successful quarterly payment, take a moment to acknowledge your efforts. A little positive reinforcement can go a long way in keeping you motivated.

5. **Plan Ahead for Major Life Changes:** If you're expecting a major life change, such as getting married, buying a house, or starting a family, plan ahead for how it will affect your taxes. These events can have a significant impact on your tax situation, so adjust your savings and estimated payments accordingly.

6. **Educate Yourself:** The more you know about taxes, the better equipped you'll be to manage them. Take the time to educate yourself on tax laws, deductions, and credits that apply to freelancers. The IRS website, tax blogs, and books on freelance finance are great resources for building your tax knowledge.

Conclusion: Saving for Taxes

Saving for taxes may not be the most exciting part of freelancing, but it's a crucial part that all freelancers must master. By setting aside money throughout the year, you're protecting yourself from financial stress, maintaining steady cash flow, and ensuring you're in compliance with the law.

With the right strategies and a proactive approach, saving for taxes can become just another part of your freelance routine – one that gives you the freedom to focus on what you love most about your work. So, start saving today, and when tax season rolls around, you'll be ready to face it with confidence and a smile!

Chapter 10: Planning for Slow Periods

> *"Saving must become a priority, not just a thought. Pay yourself first."*
> -Dave Ramsey

Imagine you're on a thrilling roller coaster ride, zooming through loops and twists at breakneck speed. But suddenly, the coaster slows down, and you find yourself creeping along, the excitement fading into a slow crawl. That's kind of like what happens in a freelance business – one moment, you're on top of the world with projects lined up, and the next, everything comes to a screeching halt. Welcome to the slow period.

Slow periods are the inevitable lull in every freelancer's career, where work isn't flowing in as quickly as you'd like, and the days seem to stretch on without a paycheck in sight. But here's the good news: with the right planning, these slow periods don't have to be scary. In fact, they can be opportunities for growth, creativity, and even relaxation – if you plan for them. So buckle up, and let's dive into why planning for slow periods is so crucial and how you can do it with style.

Why Planning for Slow Periods is a Must

Before we jump into the how-to, let's talk about the why. Why should you, as a freelancer, spend time planning for those inevitable slow periods?

Financial Stability: One of the biggest reasons to plan for slow periods is to maintain your financial stability. When work slows down, so does your income. Without a plan, you might find yourself scrambling to cover bills, rent, and other expenses. By planning ahead, you can ensure you have a financial cushion to fall back on, keeping the stress at bay and your finances intact.

Reducing Stress and Anxiety: The uncertainty of freelancing can lead to stress and anxiety, especially during slow periods. But when you've planned ahead, you can approach these lulls with confidence Knowing that you have a plan in place reduces the mental load, allowing you to stay calm and focused, even when work is scarce.

Maintaining Momentum: Slow periods don't have to mean a complete halt in your business. With a solid plan, you can use this time to work on projects that have been on the back burner, refine your skills, or explore new opportunities. Planning helps you maintain momentum and keeps your business moving forward, even when client work is slow.

Creating Opportunities: When you plan for slow periods, you're also creating opportunities for yourself. Instead of sitting idle, you can use this time to network, market your services, or develop new products. Planning turns what could be a dry spell into a period of growth and new possibilities.

Building Resilience: Freelancing is all about resilience – weathering the ups and downs with grace. By planning for slow periods, you're building your resilience muscle, learning to adapt and thrive no matter what the freelance roller coaster throws your way.

Steps to Prepare for Slow Periods

Now that we've covered the why, let's get into the how. How do you actually prepare for slow periods in your freelance business? Here are some steps to help you get started:

Create a Financial Buffer: The first step in planning for slow periods is to create a financial buffer. This is your safety net, a stash of cash set aside specifically for those times when income is low. Aim to save at least three to six months' worth of living expenses in an easily accessible account. This buffer will give you the peace of mind to weather any dry spells without financial panic.

Diversify Your Income Streams: As we discussed in a previous chapter, one way to soften the impact of slow periods is to diversify your income streams. This means having multiple sources of income, so if one stream slows down, you have others to rely on. You could offer different types of services, create passive income products like e-books or courses, or even take on part-time work in a related field. Diversifying your income makes your business more resilient and less dependent on any one source of income.

Keep Your Pipeline Full: Even when you're busy with client work, it's important to keep your pipeline full. This means constantly marketing your services, networking, and reaching out to potential clients. By keeping the momentum going, you'll be less likely to experience a sudden drop in work. Make it a habit to spend a little time each week on business development, so you're always cultivating new opportunities.

Plan Your Budget Wisely: Budgeting isn't just for the high-income months – it's crucial for planning for slow periods too. Create a budget that accounts for both your busy times and your slow times. This might mean cutting back on non-essential expenses during slower periods or adjusting your spending habits to accommodate the fluctuations in your income. A well-thought-out budget ensures you can maintain your lifestyle even when work is slow.

Use Slow Periods for Skill Development: Slow periods are the perfect time to invest in yourself. Use this time to learn new skills, take courses, or work on personal projects that can enhance your portfolio. By staying proactive, you're not only improving your skills but also increasing your value to future clients. This can lead to higher-paying opportunities when the work picks up again.

Evaluate and Adjust Your Services: Take advantage of slow periods to evaluate your services. Are there any offerings that aren't performing as well as you'd like? Are there new services you could introduce that align with current market trends? Use this time to fine-tune your business and ensure your services are meeting the needs of your clients.

Action Steps to Get Started

Ready to start planning for slow periods? Here are some action steps to help you get started:

Set Up an Emergency Fund: If you haven't already, start building your financial buffer today. Open a separate savings account and set up automatic transfers from your business income. Even small, regular contributions will add up over time. One of the things I do in my freelance business is every time I get paid for a project, in addition to taking out the percentage for taxes from the payment, I also take a set percentage, usually between 5-10%, out and deposit it into a separate 'Emergency Fund' account. This way I am constantly building my emergency fund regularly and it doesn't get forgotten about.

Audit Your Services: Take a close look at your current services and income streams. Are there any gaps or opportunities for diversification? Consider adding new offerings that complement your existing services or exploring passive income options.

Create a Marketing Plan: Develop a simple marketing plan that outlines your strategy for keeping your pipeline full. This might include regular networking events, social media outreach, or targeted email campaigns. Consistency is key, so make it a habit to market your business regularly.

Budget for the Lean Months: Review your budget and adjust it to account for potential slow periods. Identify areas where you can cut back or save more during busy times, so you're prepared when income dips.

Set Goals for Skill Development: Identify a skill or area of knowledge you'd like to improve and set a goal to work on it during your next slow period. This could be anything from learning a new software program to taking an online course in a relevant subject.

Tips and Tricks for Thriving During Slow Periods

Slow periods don't have to be a drag. Here are some tips and tricks to help you make the most of your downtime:

1. **Network Like a Pro:** Use slow periods to build and strengthen your network. Reach out to past clients, attend industry events, or join online communities related to your field. Networking can lead to new opportunities and keep you top of mind when clients need your services again.

2. **Create Content:** If you're not busy with client work, use this time to create content that showcases your expertise. Write blog posts, create videos, or update your portfolio. Content creation not only keeps you engaged but also helps attract new clients.

3. **Explore New Markets:** Slow periods are a great time to explore new markets or

niches. Consider expanding your services to a different industry or geographic area. Research potential opportunities and tailor your marketing efforts to reach new audiences.

4. **Take Care of Yourself:** Don't forget to take care of your physical and mental health during slow periods. Use the extra time to recharge, whether that means taking a vacation, practicing mindfulness, or simply enjoying some downtime. A well-rested freelancer is a more productive and creative one.

5. **Reflect and Reassess:** Use slow periods as a time for relaxation. Assess your business, your goals, and your overall satisfaction with your freelance career. Are you headed in the right direction? Are there changes you'd like to make? Reflection can help you stay aligned with your long-term vision.

6. **Stay Positive and Patient:** Slow periods are a natural part of the freelance journey. Instead of viewing them as setbacks, see them as opportunities to grow, learn, and improve. Stay positive, be patient, and trust that the work will pick up again.

Conclusion: Embrace the Slow Periods – They're Your Secret Weapon!

Slow periods may seem daunting at first, but with the right planning, they can become your secret weapon in the freelance game. By preparing financially, staying proactive, and using your downtime wisely, you'll not only survive the lulls but thrive through them.

So, the next time your freelance roller coaster slows down, don't panic. Embrace the pause, plan ahead, and turn it into an opportunity for growth, creativity, and even a little relaxation. After all, every roller coaster needs a breather before the next big thrill!

Chapter 11: Keeping Your Finger on the Pulse of Industry Trends

> *"The only place where success comes before work is in the dictionary."*
> -Vidal Sassoon, British-American hairstylist, businessman, and philanthropist

Picture this: You're cruising down the highway, wind in your hair, feeling unstoppable. But suddenly, you take a wrong turn because you didn't check the latest road updates. Now, you're lost, and that smooth ride has turned into a bumpy detour. That's what freelancing can feel like if you're not keeping an eye on industry trends. The world is constantly changing, and as a freelancer, it's your job to stay ahead of the curve. Monitoring industry trends isn't just a nice-to-have—it's a must-do if you want to stay relevant, competitive, and thriving.

In this chapter, we'll dive into why monitoring industry trends is so crucial for freelancers, how to do it without getting overwhelmed, and some actionable steps and tips to make trend-watching a fun and fruitful part of your freelance routine. Let's get started, shall we?

Why Monitoring Industry Trends is a Freelancer's Secret Weapon

First things first, why should you care about industry trends? Isn't it enough to just focus on your work and let the trends take care of themselves? Not quite. Here's why keeping tabs on the latest trends is like having a secret weapon in your freelance arsenal:

Staying Relevant: The freelance market is competitive, and it's constantly evolving. New tools, technologies, and methodologies are emerging all the time. If you're not staying up-to-date, you risk becoming outdated. Clients want to work with freelancers who are on the cutting edge, who know what's hot and what's not. By monitoring industry trends, you ensure that your skills and services remain relevant and in demand.

Spotting Opportunities: Trends often reveal new opportunities that you can capitalize on. Maybe there's a rising demand for a specific skill set you already have, or perhaps a new market is emerging that aligns perfectly with your expertise. By keeping an eye on trends, you can spot these opportunities early and position yourself as a go-to expert in that area.

Anticipating Changes: The freelance world can be unpredictable, and industries can change overnight. Whether it's a shift in client needs, a new regulation, or a technological breakthrough, being aware of trends allows you to anticipate changes before they hit. This gives you the chance to adapt, pivot, and stay ahead of the competition.

Enhancing Your Services: Monitoring trends isn't just about keeping up—it's about leveling up. By staying informed, you can continuously enhance your services, offering clients more value and staying ahead of the competition. Whether it's incorporating new tools, adopting innovative practices, or refining your processes, trend-watching helps you deliver top-notch services that clients love.

Building Credibility: When you're well-versed in the latest industry trends, you become a trusted resource for your clients. They'll look to you not just as a service provider but as an expert who can guide them through the ever-changing landscape of their industry. This builds your credibility and can lead to more referrals, repeat business, and higher rates.

How to Monitor Industry Trends Without Getting Overwhelmed

Now that you know why monitoring industry trends is so important, let's talk about how to do it effectively—without feeling like you're drowning in information. The key is to be strategic and intentional about your trend-watching efforts. Here's how:

Identify Key Sources: The first step is to identify the key sources of information in your industry. This might include industry publications, blogs, podcasts, social media accounts, and newsletters. Choose a handful of reliable sources that consistently deliver high-quality, relevant content. By narrowing your focus to a few trusted sources, you can avoid information overload and stay up-to-date without spending hours sifting through irrelevant content.

Set Up Alerts and Feeds: Automation is your friend when it comes to monitoring trends. Set up Google Alerts for specific keywords related to your industry, and use RSS feeds to aggregate content from your favorite blogs and websites. This way, you'll get the latest news and updates delivered straight to your inbox, saving you time and effort.

Join Industry Communities: Online communities and forums are goldmines for trend-watching. Join LinkedIn groups, Reddit forums, or specialized online communities where industry professionals gather to discuss the latest trends and share insights. Engaging in these communities allows you to learn from others, ask questions, and stay informed about what's happening in your field.

Follow Thought Leaders: Thought leaders and influencers in your industry are often the first to spot and discuss emerging trends. Follow them on social media, subscribe to their newsletters, and read their blogs. By keeping tabs on what these experts are saying, you'll gain valuable insights and stay ahead of the curve.

Attend Webinars and Conferences: Virtual and in-person events like webinars, conferences, and workshops are great places to learn about the latest trends and connect with other professionals in your industry. Make it a habit to attend these events regularly—they're not only educational but also great for networking.

Schedule Regular Check-Ins: Instead of trying to stay on top of trends every day, set aside specific times each week or month to catch up on the latest developments. This could be a Friday afternoon ritual or a monthly "trend check-in" where you review the latest news and updates. By dedicating regular time to trend-watching, you can stay informed without feeling overwhelmed.

Action Steps to Get Started

Ready to start monitoring industry trends like a pro? Here are some action steps to help you get started:

Create a Trend-Watching Routine: Decide on a regular schedule for monitoring industry trends. This could be a daily, weekly, or monthly routine, depending on your availability and the pace of your industry. Set aside specific time slots in your calendar for catching up on the latest news and updates.

Curate Your Information Sources: Identify the top sources of information in your industry and curate a list of go-to resources. This could include websites, blogs, podcasts, social media accounts, and newsletters. Consider using a tool like Feedly to aggregate content from multiple sources into one easy-to-read feed.

Set Up Google Alerts: Go to Google Alerts and set up alerts for specific keywords related to your industry. For example, if you're a freelance graphic designer, you might set up alerts for terms like "graphic design trends," "UI/UX," or "visual storytelling." This will ensure that you receive relevant news and updates directly in your inbox.

Join an Industry Community: Find and join at least one online community or forum related to your industry. Engage with other members, participate in discussions, and share your own insights. This will help you stay informed and build relationships with other professionals in your field.

Follow Thought Leaders: Make a list of key thought leaders and influencers in your industry and follow them on social media. Subscribe to their newsletters, read their blogs, and engage with their content. This will help you stay informed about the latest trends and gain valuable insights from industry experts.

Tips and Tricks for Effective Trend-Watching

Here are some additional tips and tricks to help you stay on top of industry trends without feeling overwhelmed:

1. **Be Selective**: With so much information out there, it's easy to get overwhelmed.

Be selective about the sources you follow and the content you consume. Focus on quality over quantity, and prioritize the information that is most relevant to your business.

2. **Keep a Trend Journal**: Consider keeping a trend journal where you jot down notes, insights, and ideas related to industry trends. This could be a physical notebook or a digital document where you record key takeaways from articles, webinars, and discussions. Reviewing your journal regularly can help you spot patterns and identify emerging opportunities.

3. **Stay Curious**: Approach trend-watching with a curious mindset. Instead of seeing it as a chore, view it as an opportunity to learn and grow. Stay open to new ideas, and don't be afraid to explore trends that are outside your comfort zone. You never know where your next big idea might come from!

4. **Network with Peers**: Don't underestimate the power of networking. Regularly connect with peers in your industry to share insights and discuss trends. Whether it's through online communities, networking events, or casual coffee chats, learning from others can provide valuable perspectives and keep you informed.

5. **Take Action**: Don't just observe trends—act on them! If you notice a trend that could benefit your business, take proactive steps to incorporate it into your services or processes. Whether it's adopting a new tool, learning a new skill, or launching a new offering, acting on trends can give you a competitive edge.

6. **Balance Trend-Watching with Focus**: While staying informed is important, it's equally important to stay focused on your core business. Don't get so caught up in chasing trends that you lose sight of what you do best. Find a balance between staying current and staying true to your unique strengths and expertise.

Conclusion: Stay Ahead by Staying Informed

In the fast-paced world of freelancing, staying ahead of the curve means staying informed. By monitoring industry trends, you can ensure that your skills and services remain relevant, spot new opportunities before they become mainstream, and build credibility as an expert in your field.

So, make trend-watching a regular part of your freelance routine. Approach it with curiosity, stay selective about your sources, and most importantly, take action on what you learn. The more informed you are, the better equipped you'll be to navigate the ever-changing landscape of freelancing and keep your business thriving.

Remember, the road to freelance success is always under construction—staying informed about industry trends is your roadmap to navigating it with confidence and flair!

Chapter 12: The Freelancer's Tax Treasure Hunt

"You don't always win, but every time you lose, you get better." -Ian Somerhalder, American actor, model, activist, director

Ah, taxes—the word that can make even the most seasoned freelancer break out in a cold sweat. But what if I told you that taxes don't have to be the nightmare you dread every April? In fact, they can be your best friend—or at least a friendly acquaintance—when you know how to take advantage of tax deductions. Imagine turning that dreaded tax bill into a manageable, maybe even pleasant, experience. Sounds good, right? Well, it's all possible when you keep abreast of tax deductions.

In this chapter, we'll explore why staying on top of tax deductions is crucial for freelancers, highlight some of the most important and common deductions you should know about, and provide actionable steps to ensure you're not leaving money on the table. We'll also throw in some tips and tricks to make tax time less of a hassle and more of a triumph. Ready? Let's dive in!

Why Keeping Abreast of Tax Deductions is a Must for Freelancers

Before we get into the nitty-gritty of deductions, let's talk about why it's so important to stay informed about them in the first place. As a freelancer, you're essentially running your own business, and that comes with a host of financial responsibilities—taxes being a big one. But here's the good news: staying informed about tax deductions can save you a significant amount of money. Here's why it's a game-changer:

Maximize Your Savings: Tax deductions reduce your taxable income, which means you pay less in taxes. By keeping track of all the deductions you're eligible for, you can significantly reduce your tax bill. It's like finding hidden treasure—every deduction is money you get to keep in your pocket.

Avoid Overpaying: If you're not aware of the deductions available to you, there's a good chance you're overpaying on your taxes. The tax code is complex, but that complexity is filled with opportunities for savings. Staying informed ensures you're not giving more money to the IRS than necessary.

Stay Compliant: The IRS expects freelancers to follow the rules, but those rules are constantly changing. By keeping up with the latest tax laws and deductions, you ensure that you're staying compliant and avoiding potential penalties or audits.

Plan for the Future: Knowing your deductions helps you plan your finances better. If you're aware of the deductions you can take, you can make smarter business decisions throughout the year—like deciding when to purchase new equipment or how to structure your expenses.

Reduce Stress: Let's face it, taxes can be stressful. But when you're informed and prepared, that stress melts away. Knowing your deductions and having a plan in place makes tax time a breeze instead of a battle.

The Most Important and Common Tax Deductions for Freelancers

Now that we've covered the "why," let's get into the "what." What are some of the most important and common tax deductions that freelancers should be aware of? Here's a rundown of the big ones:

Home Office Deduction: If you work from home, you may be eligible for the home office deduction. This allows you to deduct a portion of your rent or mortgage, utilities, and other related expenses. The key here is that the space you're claiming must be used exclusively for business purposes.

Health Insurance Premiums: As a freelancer, you're likely responsible for your own health insurance. The good news is that health insurance premiums are deductible if you're self-employed and not eligible for a group health plan through a spouse.

Business Equipment and Supplies: Any equipment or supplies you purchase for your business—think computers, software, office supplies, etc.—are deductible. This is where it pays to keep track of every little purchase, as they can add up quickly.

Internet and Phone Bills: If you use your internet and phone for business purposes, you can deduct a portion of these bills. Just be sure to only deduct the percentage that is used for business, as personal use is not deductible.

Travel Expenses: If you travel for work, whether it's to meet clients, attend conferences, or visit a worksite, those travel expenses are deductible. This includes transportation, lodging, and even a portion of your meals while on the road.

Continuing Education: Freelancers often need to stay on top of their game by learning new skills. The cost of continuing education, such as courses, workshops, and certifications related to your business, is deductible.

Advertising and Marketing: Any money you spend to promote your business—whether it's on social media ads, a new website, or business cards—is deductible. This is a big one, especially if you're actively working to grow your freelance business.

Professional Services: If you hire an accountant, lawyer, or even a virtual assistant to help with your business, those expenses are deductible. Professional services can be a big help, especially around tax time!

Bank Fees and Interest: If you have a business bank account, any fees associated with that account are deductible. The same goes for interest on business loans or credit cards.

Retirement Contributions: Contributions to a retirement plan, like a SEP IRA or Solo 401(k), are deductible. This is a win-win because you're saving for your future while also reducing your taxable income.

Action Steps to Keep on Top of Tax Deductions

So, how do you make sure you're not missing out on any of these valuable deductions? Here are some actionable steps to get you started:

Keep Detailed Records: The key to maximizing your deductions is good record-keeping. Keep track of all your expenses, no matter how small, and categorize them as you go. Use apps like QuickBooks, FreshBooks, or even a simple spreadsheet to stay organized.

Save Receipts: Always save your receipts, whether they're physical or digital. Having proof of your expenses is crucial in case you're ever audited. Consider using a receipt management app to digitize and organize your receipts.

Work with a Tax Professional: Tax laws are complex and constantly changing. Working with a tax professional who understands freelance taxes can save you time, stress, and money. They can help you identify deductions you might not have thought of and ensure you're staying compliant with the latest tax laws.

Review Your Expenses Regularly: Don't wait until tax time to review your expenses. Set aside time each month to go through your expenses and make sure everything is categorized correctly. This will make tax season much easier and less stressful.

Educate Yourself: While working with a tax professional is important, it's also a good idea to educate yourself about tax deductions. Read up on the latest tax laws, take a tax workshop for freelancers, or even just spend some time browsing the IRS website. The more you know, the better prepared you'll be.

Plan for Taxes Throughout the Year: Don't wait until April to think about taxes. Set aside money for taxes throughout the year, and make estimated tax payments if necessary. This will help you avoid a big tax bill at the end of the year.

Tips and Tricks for Maximizing Your Tax Deductions

Finally, here are some tips and tricks to help you make the most of your tax deductions:

1. **Use Accounting Software**: Invest in good accounting software that can track your income, expenses, and deductions automatically. This will save you time and ensure that nothing falls through the cracks.

2. **Track Your Mileage**: If you use your car for business purposes, track your mileage. There are apps like MileIQ that can automatically track your business mileage for you, making it easy to claim the deduction.

3. **Consider Batching Expenses**: If you know you're going to have a particularly good year income-wise, consider batching some of your expenses. For example, if you plan to buy new equipment, consider making the purchase before the end of the year to take advantage of the deduction.

4. **Maximize Retirement Contributions**: Don't forget about retirement contributions. Not only are they a great way to save for the future, but they're also tax-deductible. Max out your contributions if you can.

5. **Stay Organized**: The more organized you are, the easier it will be to maximize your deductions. Keep all your financial documents in one place, and use tools and apps to stay on top of your expenses throughout the year.

Conclusion: Turning Tax Time into Savings Time

Taxes don't have to be a source of stress—they can be a source of savings. By staying informed about tax deductions and taking proactive steps throughout the year, you can significantly reduce your tax bill and keep more of your hard-earned money in your pocket.

Remember, as a freelancer, you have the power to control your financial destiny. By keeping good records, working with a tax professional, and staying on top of your deductions, you can turn tax time into savings time. So go forth, embrace the tax code, and make the most of every deduction available to you. Your future self (and your bank account) will thank you!

Chapter 13: The Fine Print Finesse

> *"**D**on't be intimidated by what you don't know. That can be your greatest strength and ensure that you do things differently from everyone else."* -Sara Blakely, founder of Spanx

Contracts. Just the word alone might conjure up images of endless legal jargon, fine print that requires a magnifying glass, and that ever-so-dull monotone voice reading it aloud in your head. But here's the thing: mastering the art of reviewing contracts is like having a superpower in the world of freelancing. It's not just about avoiding potential pitfalls; it's about protecting your business, your time, and your hard-earned money.

In this chapter, we're going to dive into why reviewing contracts carefully is crucial for freelancers, highlight some of the most important elements to look out for, and provide actionable steps to ensure you're not signing on to something you'll regret. We'll also sprinkle in some tips and tricks to make contract reviewing less of a chore and more of a savvy business move. Ready to unleash your contract superpower? Let's go!

Why Reviewing Contracts Carefully is Non-Negotiable

Contracts are the backbone of any professional agreement—they're the written proof of what you and your client have agreed upon. But beyond just being a formality, contracts serve several crucial purposes for freelancers:

Protect Your Interests: A well-reviewed contract ensures that your rights and interests are protected. It's your safeguard against misunderstandings, scope creep, and payment disputes. By taking the time to carefully review the contract, you're setting clear expectations and protecting your business from potential headaches down the road.

Clarify the Scope of Work: Contracts clearly outline the scope of work, including what's expected of you and what's outside the agreed-upon deliverables. This clarity helps prevent scope creep, where a project's requirements start to expand beyond what was initially agreed upon without additional compensation.

Establish Payment Terms: Contracts detail how and when you'll be paid, what happens in case of late payments, and any contingencies if the project goes off course. This ensures that you're not left chasing payments or working without compensation.

Define Deliverables and Deadlines: Clear deliverables and deadlines prevent any confusion about what's expected and when. This helps manage client expectations and ensures that both parties are on the same page throughout the project.

Set Legal Protections: Contracts often include legal protections, such as confidentiality agreements, intellectual property rights, and clauses that limit your liability. These elements are vital to safeguarding your business in case something goes wrong.

Provide a Reference Point: If there's ever a dispute or confusion about the project, the contract serves as a reference point. It's the document that you can turn to in order to resolve disagreements and clarify any misunderstandings.

What to Look Out for When Reviewing Contracts

So, what exactly should you be looking for when you're handed a contract? Here are some of the most important and common things that freelancers need to keep an eye on:

Scope of Work: The scope of work section should clearly outline what you're expected to deliver. Look for specific details, such as the number of revisions, the type of deliverables, and any services that are explicitly excluded. If the scope of work is too vague, you're opening the door to potential scope creep.

Payment Terms: This is the section where you'll find the details on how much you're being paid, when you'll be paid, and how payments will be handled. Look out for red flags, such as long payment terms (e.g., 60 days) or clauses that allow the client to withhold payment for any reason. Also, check for penalties for late payments and whether you'll be reimbursed for expenses.

Deadlines and Deliverables: Make sure the contract clearly states the deadlines for each deliverable and whether there are any penalties for missing those deadlines. This is crucial for managing your time and ensuring that the project stays on track.

Ownership of Work: Intellectual property rights can be a tricky area. The contract should specify who owns the rights to the work you produce. In most cases, clients will want to own the final deliverables, but you should retain the rights to the work until you've been fully compensated. Be wary of clauses that require you to transfer ownership before payment.

Confidentiality and Non-Disclosure Agreements (NDAs): Many clients will require you to sign a confidentiality agreement or NDA, especially if you're working with sensitive information. Make sure you understand the terms and that they're reasonable. NDAs should protect the client's information without being overly restrictive.

Termination Clauses: The termination clause outlines how either party can end the contract and what happens in case of early termination. Look out for clauses that allow the client to terminate the contract without notice or without compensation for work completed. Ideally, the contract should include a notice period and compensation for any work done up to the point of termination.

Liability and Indemnity: This section outlines what happens if something goes wrong, such as a lawsuit or a project failure. Be cautious of clauses that require you to take on unlimited liability or indemnify the client for any losses. It's important that your liability is limited to the amount of the contract and that you're not held responsible for issues beyond your control.

Dispute Resolution: This clause specifies how disputes will be handled, whether through mediation, arbitration, or the court system. Ideally, disputes should be resolved through a method that's fair, cost-effective, and convenient for both parties.

Governing Law: The governing law clause states which state or country's laws will be used to interpret the contract. This is especially important if you're working with international clients, as the laws of their country may differ significantly from your own.

Amendment Clause: Contracts should include an amendment clause that specifies how changes to the contract can be made. Typically, this requires both parties to agree in writing to any changes, which helps prevent misunderstandings or unauthorized modifications.

Action Steps to Review Contracts Like a Pro

Now that you know what to look out for, here's how you can review contracts with confidence:

Take Your Time: Never rush through a contract. Set aside time to review it carefully, and don't let anyone pressure you into signing before you're ready. Remember, it's better to take a little extra time upfront than to deal with issues later on.

Read Every Word: It's tempting to skim through contracts, especially when they're filled with legal jargon, but resist the urge. Read every word, and if something isn't clear, ask for clarification. The devil is in the details, and those details could make or break your project.

Ask Questions: If you're unsure about any part of the contract, ask questions. Don't be afraid to seek clarification from the client or consult with a legal professional. It's better to ask questions now than to deal with misunderstandings later.

Negotiate Terms: Contracts are often negotiable, especially when it comes to payment terms, deadlines, and the scope of work. Don't be afraid to negotiate terms that are more favorable to you. Remember, a contract should be fair to both parties.

Consult a Legal Professional: If you're dealing with a particularly complex contract or if you're not comfortable reviewing contracts on your own, consider consulting a legal professional. They can help you understand the terms and ensure that your interests are protected.

Keep a Copy: Once you've signed the contract, make sure you keep a copy for your records. This is your reference point in case any issues arise during the project.

Tips and Tricks for Making Contract Reviewing a Breeze

Finally, here are some tips and tricks to make the process of reviewing contracts less daunting and more effective:

1. **Use a Checklist**: Create a checklist of the key elements you need to review in every contract. This will help you stay organized and ensure that you don't overlook anything important.

2. **Automate with Templates**: If you find yourself creating or reviewing contracts frequently, consider using templates. You can create your own template that includes your preferred terms and conditions, which you can use as a starting point for negotiations.

3. **Stay Organized**: Keep all your contracts in one place, whether it's a physical folder or a digital file. This makes it easy to reference them when needed and ensures that you're always prepared.

4. **Keep Learning**: Contract law is constantly evolving, and so should your knowledge. Stay informed about the latest trends and best practices in contract management for freelancers. This will help you stay ahead of the curve and protect your business.

5. **Trust Your Gut**: If something in the contract doesn't feel right, trust your instincts. It's better to ask for changes or walk away from a bad contract than to enter into an agreement that could harm your business.

Conclusion: Turn Contracts into Confidence

Reviewing contracts might not be the most glamorous part of freelancing, but it's one of the most important. By taking the time to carefully review and understand each contract you sign, you're not just protecting your business—you're setting the stage for a successful, stress-free project.

Remember, contracts are there to protect both you and your client, and a well-reviewed contract can be the foundation of a great working relationship. So, the next time a contract lands in your inbox, don't shy away from it. Embrace it as an opportunity to flex your freelance muscles, ensure a fair agreement, and set yourself up for success. After all, when it comes to your freelance business, you deserve nothing less than the best!

Chapter 14: Your Financial GPS – Why Every Freelancer Needs a Financial Advisor

*"**The** number one reason people fail in life is because they listen to their friends, family, and neighbors."* -Napoleon Hill

Imagine setting out on a cross-country road trip without a map or GPS. Sure, you might get where you're going eventually, but it'll probably involve a few wrong turns, some dead ends, and a lot of unnecessary stress. Now, think of your freelance career as that journey and your finances as the car that's getting you there. Wouldn't it be nice to have a trusted guide to keep you on the right track, avoid the potholes, and make sure you're heading in the right direction?

Enter the financial advisor—the GPS for your financial journey. In this chapter, we'll explore why consulting a financial advisor is crucial for freelancers, delve into the top reasons to seek their expertise and provide actionable steps to get started. We'll also share some tips and tricks to make the most out of your relationship with your financial advisor. So, buckle up, and let's navigate the road to financial success together!

Why Consulting a Financial Advisor is a Game-Changer for Freelancers

Freelancing offers incredible freedom—freedom to choose your projects, set your schedule, and be your own boss. But with that freedom comes a hefty dose of responsibility, especially when it comes to managing your finances. Unlike traditional employees who have payroll departments, retirement plans, and health benefits handed to them on a silver platter, freelancers have to juggle all these financial aspects on their own. And let's be honest, not all of us are financial wizards.

This is where a financial advisor comes in. A financial advisor is more than just a money guru—they're your financial co-pilot, helping you navigate the complexities of freelance finances. Here's why consulting a financial advisor is a game-changer for freelancers:

Personalized Financial Planning: No two freelancers are alike. Your financial situation is unique, with its own set of challenges and opportunities. A financial advisor tailors their advice to your specific needs, goals, and circumstances. Whether you're just starting out or you're a seasoned freelancer, they help create a customized financial plan that fits your life.

Expert Guidance on Taxes: Taxes can be a freelancer's worst nightmare. With fluctuating income, multiple income streams, and a slew of deductions to track, it's easy to feel overwhelmed. A financial advisor helps you navigate the labyrinth of tax laws, ensuring that you're maximizing deductions, minimizing liabilities, and staying compliant with the IRS.

Retirement Planning: As a freelancer, you don't have the luxury of an employer-sponsored 401(k). Planning for retirement is entirely on your shoulders. A financial advisor helps you set up and manage retirement accounts, like IRAs or solo 401(k)s, ensuring that you're saving enough to enjoy a comfortable retirement.

Cash Flow Management: Freelancing often comes with irregular income, which can make managing cash flow tricky. A financial advisor helps you create a budget, manage your expenses, and set aside funds for slower periods, so you're not left scrambling when the cash flow slows down.

Investment Advice: Investing can be a powerful way to grow your wealth, but it's also fraught with risks. A financial advisor helps you navigate the world of investments, offering advice on where to invest, how to diversify your portfolio, and when to take risks (and when to avoid them).

Debt Management: If you're carrying debt, whether it's student loans, credit card debt, or a business loan, a financial advisor helps you create a plan to pay it off. They offer strategies to reduce interest payments, consolidate debt, and prioritize payments, so you can become debt-free faster.

Goal Setting and Accountability: One of the biggest challenges freelancers face is staying on track with their financial goals. A financial advisor helps you set realistic goals, whether it's saving for a big purchase, paying off debt, or building an emergency fund. They also hold you accountable, providing regular check-ins to ensure you're making progress.

Peace of Mind: Perhaps the most valuable benefit of consulting a financial advisor is the peace of mind that comes with knowing your finances are in good hands. Instead of stressing over money, you can focus on what you do best—your freelance work—while your advisor handles the financial details.

Top Reasons to Consult a Financial Advisor

Now that we've covered the benefits of working with a financial advisor, let's dive into some of the most common reasons freelancers seek their expertise:

Complex Financial Situations: Freelancers often have more complex financial situations than traditional employees. Multiple income streams, varying tax obligations, and the need to plan for both short-term and long-term goals can create a financial puzzle that's difficult to solve on your own. A financial advisor helps you piece it all together.

Big Life Changes: Whether you're getting married, buying a home, or starting a family, big life changes can have a significant impact on your finances. A financial advisor helps you navigate these transitions, ensuring that your financial plan adapts to your new circumstances.

Planning for the Future: Maybe you're thinking about scaling your freelance business, transitioning to a different field, or retiring early. A financial advisor helps you create a plan to achieve these long-term goals, providing guidance on savings, investments, and risk management.

Saving for Taxes: As a freelancer, you're responsible for paying quarterly estimated taxes. It can be easy to underestimate how much you need to set aside, leading to a big tax bill at the end of the year. A financial advisor helps you calculate your tax obligations and ensures that you're setting aside enough to cover them.

Reducing Financial Stress: Money worries can take a toll on your mental health and overall well-being. If you're feeling overwhelmed by your finances, a financial advisor can help you regain control and reduce stress by creating a clear plan and offering ongoing support.

Making Informed Decisions: Whether you're considering a major purchase, evaluating a new business opportunity, or thinking about investing in the stock market, a financial advisor provides the information and insights you need to make informed decisions.

Action Steps to Get Started with a Financial Advisor

Ready to bring a financial advisor on board? Here's how to get started:

Assess Your Needs: Before you start searching for a financial advisor, take some time to assess your financial needs. Are you looking for help with tax planning, retirement savings, investment advice, or all of the above? Understanding what you need will help you find the right advisor for you.

Do Your Research: Not all financial advisors are created equal. Look for advisors who specialize in working with freelancers or self-employed individuals. Check their credentials, read reviews, and ask for recommendations from other freelancers or business owners.

Schedule a Consultation: Many financial advisors offer free initial consultations. Use this opportunity to ask questions, discuss your financial goals, and get a feel for whether the advisor is a good fit for you. Don't be afraid to meet with multiple advisors before making a decision.

Check Credentials: Look for advisors who are certified and have relevant experience. Certifications like CFP (Certified Financial Planner), CPA (Certified Public Accountant), and CFA (Chartered Financial Analyst) indicate that the advisor has met rigorous professional standards.

Discuss Fees: Financial advisors charge for their services in different ways—some charge a flat fee, others charge an hourly rate, and some take a percentage of your assets under management. Make sure you understand how the advisor charges and whether their fees are within your budget.

Set Clear Expectations: Once you've chosen a financial advisor, it's important to set clear expectations from the start. Discuss how often you'll meet, what services the advisor will provide, and how you'll communicate. Setting these expectations upfront ensures a smooth working relationship.

Tips and Tricks for Working with a Financial Advisor

To make the most out of your relationship with your financial advisor, here are some tips and tricks:

1. **Be Transparent**: The more your financial advisor knows about your financial situation, the better they can help you. Be transparent about your income, expenses, debts, and financial goals. Honesty is key to building a strong working relationship.

2. **Stay Engaged**: While your financial advisor is there to guide you, it's important to stay engaged in the process. Ask questions, seek clarification, and make sure you understand the advice you're receiving. Remember, it's your financial future on the line.

3. **Review Regularly**: Your financial situation will change over time, and so should your financial plan. Schedule regular reviews with your advisor to discuss any changes in your life or goals. This ensures that your financial plan stays relevant and effective.

4. **Take Action**: Your financial advisor can provide all the advice in the world, but it's up to you to take action. Follow through on their recommendations,

whether it's setting up a retirement account, creating a budget, or investing in a new opportunity.

5. **Keep an Open Mind**: Your financial advisor may suggest strategies or investments that are outside your comfort zone. Keep an open mind and consider their advice, but also make sure you're comfortable with any decisions you make. After all, it's your money.

6. **Don't Be Afraid to Switch**: If you're not satisfied with your financial advisor, don't be afraid to make a change. Your financial well-being is too important to settle for anything less than the best. If the relationship isn't working, it's okay to move on and find someone who's a better fit.

Conclusion: Charting Your Course to Financial Freedom

Consulting a financial advisor isn't just about managing your money—it's about charting a course to financial freedom. With their expert guidance, personalized advice, and ongoing support, you can navigate the complexities of freelance finances with confidence. Whether you're just starting out or looking to take your freelance business to the next level, a financial advisor is an invaluable partner on your journey to success.

So, why go it alone when you can have a trusted co-pilot by your side? Take the first step today by consulting a financial advisor and setting yourself up for a prosperous freelance career. Your future self will thank you!

Chapter 15: Reviewing Your Financial Goals Annually

> *"If we command our wealth, we shall be rich and free. If our wealth commands us, we are poor indeed."* -Edmund Burke, Economist

As a freelancer, you're the captain of your own financial ship. You get to chart the course, set the destination, and steer the wheel. But even the best sailors need to check their bearings and adjust their course from time to time. That's where reviewing your financial goals annually comes in.

It's easy to get swept up in the day-to-day hustle of freelancing—juggling client deadlines, managing projects, and trying to grow your business. But if you don't take a step back to reflect on your financial goals, you risk drifting off course. Reviewing your goals once a year is like performing a "financial health check." It's not only about seeing how far you've come, but also making sure you're still headed in the right direction.

Let's explore why reviewing your financial goals annually is crucial for freelancers, and how you can make this process an exciting, empowering part of your freelance journey.

Why It's Important to Review Your Financial Goals Annually

Life Happens: Your Goals Will Change Life as a freelancer is unpredictable. New opportunities arise, markets shift, and your personal needs evolve. Maybe you wanted to save for a new computer this year, but now you're eyeing a down payment on a house.

Your goals should adapt to where you are in life. If you don't check in with yourself annually, you might end up working towards goals that no longer align with your true priorities. Reviewing them gives you the chance to reassess what matters most to you and adjust your plan accordingly.

Track Your Progress and Celebrate Wins Think of your annual review as a celebration. This is your moment to reflect on all the financial wins you've achieved throughout the year. Did you hit that savings target? Pay off a chunk of debt? Book a dream client? Whatever your milestones, recognizing them is key to staying motivated. Celebrating wins, big and small, will keep you energized and excited about continuing to grow your freelance business.

Stay Focused and Motivated When you review your financial goals annually, you're reminding yourself of why you're doing this freelance hustle in the first place. Having those clear targets helps you stay focused and motivated. It's easy to get sidetracked by short-term demands, but regular goal check-ins ensure that you're always moving in the direction of your long-term vision. Revisiting your financial aspirations keeps you grounded and inspired to keep pushing forward.

Identify What's Working—and What's Not Your annual financial review is also a reality check. It allows you to see which strategies are helping you reach your goals, and which might need tweaking. Maybe that budgeting system you started using worked wonders, or perhaps your plan to save for taxes fell a bit short. Reflecting on your financial successes and challenges helps you refine your approach so that next year, you can be even more effective.

How to Review Your Financial Goals: Action Steps

Now that we know why reviewing your financial goals is so important, let's break down exactly how to do it. This isn't just about looking at numbers—it's about asking yourself meaningful questions and creating an actionable plan for the next year.

Set Aside Time Make it a ritual! Choose a specific time each year—maybe at the start of the new year or at the end of your business's fiscal year—to sit down and review your goals. Block off a few hours in your calendar, pour yourself a nice cup of coffee (or tea, or wine—your choice!), and make this a dedicated, no-distractions session.

Gather Your Financial Data Pull together all the relevant info you'll need to review your finances. This includes income statements, expense reports, savings accounts, investment portfolios, and any debt you're working on paying off. If you've been using financial software, this step will be a breeze. If not, it's a good opportunity to get organized!

Reflect on the Past Year Ask yourself these key questions:

- Did I meet my financial goals? If not, why?

- What unexpected financial challenges did I face?

- Were there any financial surprises (good or bad) that I didn't anticipate?

- What strategies helped me the most?

- Where did I struggle, and what could I have done differently?

Being honest about your progress is important. If you didn't reach a particular goal, that's okay! The goal here is to understand what happened, learn from it, and refine your approach for the future.

Reassess Your Goals After reflecting on your past year, consider if your financial goals still align with your current priorities. Maybe some goals can stay as they are, while others need to be adjusted. Perhaps you've exceeded your expectations and need to set the bar higher! This is your chance to fine-tune your financial targets to ensure they reflect where you are today.

Create New Goals for the Coming Year Once you've assessed your progress and realigned your goals, it's time to set new ones for the year ahead. Aim to create S.M.A.R.T. goals—specific, measurable, achievable, relevant, and time-bound. For example, instead of saying "I want to save more," you could set a goal like, "I will save $10,000 by the end of the year by putting aside $833 each month."

Break Goals Into Actionable Steps Big goals can feel overwhelming, but breaking them down into bite-sized steps makes them manageable. If your goal is to save $10,000, break it into monthly targets. If you want to pay off a debt, calculate how much you need to contribute each week. This way, you'll always know what the next step is.

Tips and Tricks for Staying on Track

1. **Use Visual Tools** Get creative with your goal-setting! Consider using a vision board or financial tracker that you can keep visible. Seeing your goals visually every day helps keep them front of mind and makes them feel more achievable.

2. **Automate Where You Can** Automation is your friend. Set up automatic transfers to your savings account, retirement fund, or investment accounts. This way, you're consistently working toward your goals without having to think about it.

3. **Check-In Quarterly** While annual reviews are key, consider doing a quick financial check-in every quarter. This ensures you stay on track throughout the year and can make any mid-course corrections if needed.

4. **Celebrate Milestones Along the Way** Don't wait until you hit your final goal to celebrate—recognize progress at every step. Whether it's putting aside your first $1,000 or successfully negotiating a higher freelance rate, each win brings you closer to your bigger goals. Reward yourself in small ways to keep that motivation flowing.

Wrapping It Up: Your Financial Goals Are the Map to Success

Annual financial reviews aren't just about the numbers—they're about reflecting on your journey, celebrating your successes, and adjusting your course for the year ahead. As a freelancer, you have the power to shape your financial future, and by checking in with your goals each year, you stay in control of that destiny.

So, make reviewing your financial goals an exciting part of your freelance adventure. Use it as a chance to dream big, plan strategically, and set yourself up for even greater success in the future. Your goals are your roadmap—keep them updated, and you'll always know where you're headed!

Chapter 16: Building a Buffer for Life's Freelance Surprises

"Expect the best. Prepare for the worst. Capitalize on what comes." -Zig Ziglar, motivational speaker

Picture this: you're cruising along in your freelance business, clients are happy, projects are rolling in, and you're feeling unstoppable. Then, suddenly, something unexpected happens. Maybe a client ghosts you on a payment, or your laptop decides it's time for retirement, or even worse—a slow season creeps in with no new projects on the horizon. In times like these, your emergency fund becomes your life jacket, keeping you afloat and stress-free while you navigate the choppy waters of freelancing.

Building an emergency fund is one of the smartest financial moves a freelancer can make. It's not about being pessimistic; it's about being prepared. Freelancers don't have the luxury of a steady paycheck or employer-backed safety nets, so you've got to create your own. In this chapter, we're going to dive into why an emergency fund is an absolute must for every freelancer, and more importantly, how you can start building one today.

Why an Emergency Fund is Crucial for Freelancers

Freelancing is Unpredictable (and That's Okay!) Unlike traditional employees, freelancers experience peaks and valleys in income. Some months might be a feast of projects, while others could feel like a famine. It's the nature of the game. But while that unpredictability can be exciting, it can also be stressful if you're not prepared for the leaner times. An emergency fund smooths out those income bumps and ensures that you won't be scrambling when cash flow slows down.

Protect Yourself from Late Payments Let's be honest, not every client pays on time. Late payments are a real issue in the freelance world, and when you're counting on that cash to cover your bills, it can be a major source of stress. An emergency fund acts as a buffer, giving you peace of mind while you're chasing down that overdue invoice. Instead of panicking, you can calmly follow up with the client while knowing your essential expenses are covered.

Cover Unexpected Business Expenses Freelancers rely on their tools—whether that's your laptop, camera, software, or other equipment—to get the job done. But what happens when your trusty tools break down unexpectedly? Repairs and replacements aren't cheap, and they always seem to happen at the worst possible time. With an emergency fund in place, you won't have to scramble to find the cash. You'll be ready to handle any tech crisis that comes your way without missing a beat.

Health Emergencies and Personal Crises Life doesn't stop happening just because you're a freelancer. You could face a health issue that takes you out of commission for a while, or a family emergency could arise that demands your immediate attention. Without paid sick days or a team to back you up, your business could come to a screeching halt. An emergency fund provides financial protection during these personal crises, allowing you to focus on what matters most without worrying about how you'll pay the bills.

Plan for Slow Seasons Without Panic Every freelancer has experienced the dreaded "slow season." Maybe it's the holidays, or maybe it's just a lull in the market. Either way, these quiet periods are inevitable, but they don't have to be nerve-wracking. With an emergency fund, you can sail through the slow months without feeling the pressure to scramble for work or dip into your regular savings. It's a cushion that gives you breathing room, allowing you to ride out the dry spells with confidence.

How Much Should You Save in Your Emergency Fund?

Before you start building your fund, you're probably wondering, "How much do I actually need?" The answer depends on your unique situation, but a good rule of thumb for freelancers is to aim for **three to six months' worth of living expenses**. That might sound like a lot, but don't worry—we're going to break it down into manageable steps.

Action Steps to Build Your Emergency Fund

Calculate Your Monthly Expenses The first step is figuring out exactly how much you need to live on each month. This includes rent or mortgage, utilities, groceries, insurance, transportation, and any other essential costs. Add it all up, and now you've got your target monthly number.

Set a Savings Goal Now that you know your monthly expenses, you can multiply that number by 3 to 6 months to find out how much you should aim to save in your emergency fund. Don't get overwhelmed if the total feels high—it's okay to start small. The key is to just get started.

Break It Down into Smaller Goals Saving a full emergency fund all at once might feel like a mountain to climb, but breaking it down into bite-sized goals makes it way more achievable. Start by setting a mini-goal, like saving one month's worth of expenses. Once you hit that, aim for two months, and so on. Every little bit adds up over time.

Automate Your Savings One of the easiest ways to build your emergency fund is by automating your savings. Set up automatic transfers from your business income into a separate savings account dedicated to your emergency fund. You can decide on a fixed percentage of your income—say 10% or 15%—to go directly into savings each month. This way, you're consistently working toward your goal without even thinking about it.

Cut Back and Funnel Extra Cash During your journey to build your emergency fund, consider cutting back on non-essential expenses. That doesn't mean you have to give up every little joy, but maybe there are some areas where you can trim the fat. Use that extra cash to give your emergency fund a boost. Did you land a particularly big project this month? Funnel a portion of that windfall into your savings.

Tips and Tricks for Building Your Fund

1. **Keep Your Emergency Fund Separate** It's crucial to keep your emergency fund in a separate account from your everyday business and personal checking

accounts. This keeps you from dipping into it for non-emergencies and makes it easier to track your progress. Plus, seeing that fund grow over time is incredibly satisfying!

2. **Start with What You Can** You don't need to save huge chunks all at once. If all you can spare is $50 or $100 a month, start there. The important thing is to be consistent. Over time, you'll see your emergency fund grow, and those small contributions will add up faster than you think.

3. **Don't Be Afraid to Use It—But Only for True Emergencies** Your emergency fund is there for a reason, so don't hesitate to use it when you truly need it. However, it's important to distinguish between a real emergency and a "want." A new gadget might be tempting, but unless it's essential to keep your business running, it's better to leave the emergency fund untouched.

4. **Replenish It After Using It** If you do end up dipping into your emergency fund, make it a priority to rebuild it as soon as possible. Go back to saving consistently until you've replenished what you've used, so you're always prepared for the next unexpected situation.

5. **Reward Yourself Along the Way** As you reach milestones in your savings journey, don't forget to reward yourself. Hit your first $1,000? Treat yourself to something small and fun. Celebrating your progress keeps you motivated to continue saving.

Wrapping It Up: The Power of Being Prepared

Building an emergency fund might not be the flashiest part of freelancing, but it's one of the most empowering. When you have that safety net in place, you're giving yourself the freedom to weather any storm without the stress of wondering how you'll make ends meet. It's about peace of mind, security, and long-term stability.

By starting today, even with small steps, you're taking control of your financial future. And the next time life throws a curveball your way, you'll be ready—calm, collected, and confident that your emergency fund has your back.

Chapter 17: Automating Savings (Even When Your Income is Wild)

> *"It's not how much money you make, but how much money you keep, how hard it works for you, and how many generations you keep it for."*
> -Robert Kiyosaki

Imagine if every time you got paid, a portion of your income just *magically* whisked itself away into savings, without you lifting a finger. That's the beauty of automating your savings as a freelancer. No second-guessing, no guilt about how much to set aside, and no temptation to spend it all—just seamless, consistent savings that build up over time.

For freelancers, automating savings isn't just a smart financial move—it's practically a necessity. In a world where your income fluctuates from month to month, and financial priorities are constantly shifting, automation is the best way to stay on track with your goals. But what if your income is *so* unpredictable that you don't know what's coming in from month to month? Don't worry! In this chapter, we'll dive into how to make automation work for *every* freelancer—whether your income is steady or wildly erratic.

Why Automating Your Savings is Crucial for Freelancers

Eliminates Decision Fatigue: Let's face it—deciding how much to save every time you get paid can feel like a chore. Should you save more this month because you landed a big project? Or maybe less, because things are tight? Automation takes the guesswork out of the equation. Once you set it up, it runs on autopilot, saving you from having to make constant decisions about money. Your brain is freed up to focus on what you do best—crushing it in your freelance work!

Builds Consistency: Consistency is key when it comes to saving money. Freelancers, by nature, have unpredictable incomes, but that doesn't mean your savings should be inconsistent. When you automate your savings, you're ensuring that no matter how much you earn in a given month, you're still making progress toward your financial goals. It's the tortoise-and-hare situation—slow and steady wins the race. Even small amounts add up over time when they're saved regularly.

Saves You from Temptation: When money is just sitting in your checking account, it's all too easy to spend it. That extra coffee? Sure, why not. A new gadget you don't really need? It's only one click away. But when your savings are automatically whisked out of reach, you remove that temptation. You don't miss what you don't see, and you'll be less likely to dip into your savings for non-essential spending.

Helps You Weather Freelance Income Fluctuations: Some months as a freelancer can feel like you've hit the jackpot, while others can leave you wondering where the next project will come from. Automating your savings allows you to maintain a steady financial habit, no matter what your income looks like. During the high-earning months, you'll save more without even thinking about it, building up a cushion for the slower times.

Makes Reaching Financial Goals Easier: Whether you're saving for a big-ticket item like a new computer, setting aside money for taxes, or building up your emergency fund, automation makes it so much easier. By setting up automatic transfers, you're ensuring that you're always moving closer to your goals without having to manually move the money yourself. You get to fast-track your progress while still feeling like you're on cruise control.

How to Automate Your Savings –

Step-by-Step

Pick a Savings Goal: First things first—what are you saving for? This could be a rainy-day fund, your tax obligations, a new piece of equipment, or even retirement. Having a clear goal in mind will motivate you to keep that automation running smoothly. You can even set up multiple savings automations for different goals, so each one is getting the attention it deserves.

Open a Separate Savings Account: To keep your savings on track, it's smart to open a separate account just for your automated transfers. This makes it harder to dip into those funds accidentally or out of temptation. Many banks offer high-interest savings accounts or dedicated accounts specifically for freelancers. Find one that works for you and your goals.

Choose an Amount to Automate: Now comes the fun part—deciding how much to automate. If your income is fairly predictable, you can choose a flat dollar amount to automatically transfer into your savings each month. But what if your income is erratic? This is where it gets interesting! Instead of setting a fixed amount, consider automating a percentage of your income. For example, if you automate 10% of every invoice, you'll save more in the months when business is booming and less during leaner times. The key is to create a system that adapts to your cash flow without stressing you out.

Set Up Automatic Transfers: Most banks and financial apps make it easy to set up automatic transfers. Choose how often you want to transfer money (weekly, bi-weekly, or monthly), and set it to go from your checking account into your savings account. If your income fluctuates wildly, you might want to sync your transfers with when you get paid. For instance, if you get paid sporadically, you can set up the transfer to happen a day after you receive payment. That way, it's always aligned with your incoming cash flow.

Monitor and Adjust as Needed: Freelance businesses are always evolving, so your savings plan should be flexible too. Periodically check in on your automated transfers and make adjustments as needed. Did you just land a big retainer client? Maybe it's time to increase your savings percentage. Conversely, if you're going through a slower period, it's okay to scale back until things pick up again. The key is to make automation work for your current situation.

What to Do If Your Income is Too Erratic to Automate Savings

If your income is highly unpredictable, automating savings might feel daunting—but it's still possible! Here's how to make it work:

Save After Every Payment: Instead of automating a specific amount every month, try automating a percentage of every payment you receive. That way, even if you only get paid once or twice a month, you'll still be putting money aside consistently. If you can, aim for 10% of every invoice, but adjust that percentage based on your needs and comfort level.

Use Windfall Savings: In months when you receive a larger-than-expected payment, consider transferring a bigger chunk of that income into savings. For example, if you land a high-paying project, you could transfer 30% of that payment into savings, giving yourself a nice financial cushion for leaner months.

Manual Top-Ups: If automating savings feels unrealistic during lean periods, take a manual approach. Every time you receive payment, assess what's available and manually transfer an appropriate amount into your savings. While this isn't fully automated, you can make it a habit by doing it on a set schedule—say, every Friday or the last day of each month.

Budget Buffering: Create a buffer account specifically for months when income is slow. By manually transferring money into this buffer account during busy months, you can draw from it when times are lean, helping you stay consistent in your savings efforts without feeling the pinch.

Action Steps to Start Automating Your Savings

Decide on a Savings Goal – Write down what you're saving for and how much you want to accumulate. This will keep you motivated to stick with your savings plan.

Choose a Savings Account – Open a dedicated savings account if you don't have one already. Ideally, go for one with no fees and some interest.

Set Up Automatic Transfers – Use your bank's automatic transfer feature or an app to start moving money into your savings account on a regular

Tips and Tricks for Automating Your Savings

1. **Use Multiple Accounts for Different Goals** One clever trick is to open multiple savings accounts for different goals. For instance, you could have one account for your tax savings, one for your emergency fund, and another for that dream vacation. This helps you track progress for each goal and ensures that every dollar has a purpose. Many online banks make it easy to open multiple accounts with no fees, so take advantage of this option!

2. **Leverage Apps to Help You Automate** There are tons of apps designed to make saving money easier, especially for freelancers. Tools like Qapital, Digit, and Simple can automatically move small amounts into savings based on your spending habits or round up your purchases to the nearest dollar and save the difference. Think of it as automating your automation—it's double the power for building your savings!

3. **Treat It Like a Bill** One of the best ways to commit to saving is to treat it like a non-negotiable bill. Just like you wouldn't skip paying your rent or electricity, don't skip your savings. When you prioritize it this way, it becomes a habit, and you'll feel good about checking it off your financial to-do list each month.

4. **Celebrate Your Milestones** Automating your savings doesn't mean you can't enjoy the process. Set small milestones for yourself, and when you hit them, celebrate! Reached your first $1,000? Treat yourself to something fun (within reason, of course). The more you enjoy the process, the more motivated you'll be to keep saving.

5. **Don't Forget About Retirement Savings** Automation isn't just for short-term goals. Freelancers need to plan for the long haul too, and that includes retirement. Set up automated contributions to a retirement account like an IRA or SEP-IRA. This way, you're not only building savings for today but also investing in your future. I'll cover this in more detail in the next chapter.

Wrapping It Up: The Freedom of Automating Your Savings

Automating your savings isn't just a financial hack—it's a freelancing superpower. It allows you to effortlessly build up funds for both short-term goals and long-term security without the stress of manual decisions. By taking that step today, you're freeing up mental space, reducing the temptation to overspend, and giving yourself the consistency needed to hit your financial targets.

With every automatic transfer, you're inching closer to financial freedom—without lifting a finger. Now, that's the kind of magic every freelancer deserves.

Chapter 18: From Gig to Golden Years

"It's better to look ahead and prepare than to look back and regret." -Jackie Joyner-Kersee

Freelancing offers boundless freedom — the ability to choose your clients, set your own rates, work when you want, and even work from wherever you desire. But with great freedom comes great responsibility, and one of the most overlooked responsibilities for freelancers is planning for retirement.

If you're employed in a traditional job, you might be used to company-sponsored retirement plans, automatic contributions, and an HR department reminding you to stash away part of your paycheck for the future. But for freelancers? You're your own HR department, finance officer, and CEO. Planning for retirement can feel like a distant concern, but trust me, it's essential to your long-term success and happiness.

Why Freelancers Need to Think About Retirement Now

In the hustle and bustle of the freelance life — meeting deadlines, managing clients, juggling finances — it's easy to push thoughts of retirement aside. You might think, "I'll deal with that later when I'm earning more," or "I love what I do, so why would I retire?" But here's the kicker: *later* can sneak up on you fast.

Retirement planning isn't just about quitting work. It's about building financial security so that when you want to slow down, focus on passion projects, or, yes, take time off without worrying about paying the bills, you have that option. Without a well-thought-out retirement plan, you might find yourself working long past the time you would have preferred to relax and enjoy the fruits of your labor.

Consider this: as a freelancer, you don't have the luxury of pension plans, employer contributions, or automatic retirement savings. It's up to you to create your own nest egg, and the earlier you start, the better off you'll be.

The Tale of Two Freelancers

Let's dive into the stories of two freelancers: Sara and Mark.

Sara's Smart Start Sara began freelancing as a graphic designer in her mid-20s. After a few years of solidifying her client base and figuring out the ups and downs of freelance income, she realized she needed to think about retirement. With no employer to set up a 401(k), Sara decided to take matters into her own hands.

She set up a **Solo 401(k)** (more on this later!) and committed to contributing a percentage of every payment she received. No matter how small or large the job, she ensured that at least 10% went into her retirement fund. Over time, as her income grew, she increased her contributions. Thanks to compound interest, Sara's retirement savings began to grow at a steady pace. Now, in her mid-40s, she's on track to retire comfortably, even though she still loves her work and may never fully "retire."

Mark's Missed Opportunity Mark, on the other hand, started his freelance writing business in his 30s. He made good money and loved the flexibility his work gave him. But whenever someone mentioned retirement planning, he would brush it off. "I'll deal with it next year," he'd say.

Fast forward to Mark's 50th birthday, and the reality hit him hard. Without any savings, no employer-sponsored plan, and inconsistent income, Mark found himself scrambling to set aside funds for the future. He had to drastically increase his workload and cut down on expenses to make up for lost time. Retirement was no longer an option — he needed to work just to survive.

Sara and Mark's stories demonstrate the difference that early planning can make. Retirement is not something you want to leave to chance, and it's certainly not something you should procrastinate on.

Creating Your Own Freelance Retirement Package

Now that you're motivated to plan, let's talk about how to create your own freelance retirement package. It might sound daunting, but it's easier than you think once you know the options available.

Solo 401(k) A Solo 401(k) is a retirement account designed for self-employed individuals. One of the biggest benefits of this plan is the high contribution limit, which allows you to contribute as both the employee and the employer. In 2024, for example, you can contribute up to $22,500 as an employee (or $30,000 if you're over 50) and an additional amount as an employer, up to a total of $66,000. The best part? These contributions reduce your taxable income, helping you save on taxes while building your retirement fund.

SEP IRA (Simplified Employee Pension IRA) A SEP IRA is another great option for freelancers. With a SEP IRA, you can contribute up to 25% of your net earnings from self-employment, up to a maximum of $66,000. SEP IRAs are easy to set up, and contributions are tax-deductible, making them a flexible and tax-efficient way to save for retirement.

Roth IRA A Roth IRA allows you to contribute after-tax dollars, meaning you don't get a tax deduction now, but your money grows tax-free, and you won't have to pay taxes when you withdraw in retirement. The contribution limit for 2024 is $6,500 ($7,500 if you're over 50), but it's a great supplement to a Solo 401(k) or SEP IRA.

Automate Your Contributions Just like we talked about automating your savings, automating your retirement contributions is a fantastic way to stay on track. Set up automatic transfers from your checking account to your retirement account, so you never have to think twice about saving for the future.

What If Your Income Is Erratic?

If you're like many freelancers, your income may fluctuate from month to month. In this case, planning for retirement can feel especially tricky. The key here is flexibility.

Start by contributing a consistent percentage of your income. Even if you have a lean month, contributing something — even if it's small — will keep you in the habit of saving for retirement. In months when your income is higher, make a point to contribute more. The important thing is to avoid going long periods without putting something away for the future.

Another strategy for managing erratic income is creating a **buffer fund** that smooths out your monthly savings. This fund acts as a cushion, allowing you to maintain steady retirement contributions, even during slow periods.

Tips and Tricks for Successful Retirement Planning

1. **Start Now:** It doesn't matter if you're 25 or 45; the best time to start saving for retirement is now. The earlier you start, the more time your money has to grow.

2. **Contribute Regularly:** Whether it's a percentage of your earnings or a fixed dollar amount, the key to successful retirement savings is consistency.

3. **Maximize Your Contributions:** Aim to contribute the maximum allowed to your retirement accounts, especially if you have a good year. Take advantage of the tax benefits and build your future nest egg.

4. **Seek Financial Advice:** Retirement planning can be complex, especially with fluctuating freelance income. If you're unsure which plan is best for you or how much to contribute, consulting with a financial advisor can help you avoid mistakes and maximize your retirement savings.

The Importance of Professional Help

Freelancers wear many hats, and managing your retirement planning is a huge responsibility. While many freelancers are perfectly capable of setting up their retirement plans, others may find it beneficial to seek out a financial advisor. A professional can help you choose the right retirement plan, determine how much you should be saving based on your unique situation, and adjust your strategy as your business grows.

After all, there's no one-size-fits-all approach to retirement planning. Whether you want to retire early, work part-time during retirement, or simply ensure financial security, a financial advisor can help you create a plan that works for you.

The Road to Retirement Starts Now

Retirement may seem far away, but it's never too early (or too late) to start planning for it. As a freelancer, you're in control of your income, your work, and your financial future. Building a strong retirement fund is one of the most important investments you can make in yourself and your future freedom. Follow the steps, seek advice when needed, and start planning now. Your future self will thank you!

Chapter 19: Freelance Perks: Crafting Your Own Benefits Plan

> *"Money, like emotions, is something you must control to keep your life on the right track."* -Natasha Munson

Freelancing comes with an undeniable sense of freedom: no bosses, no strict schedules, and the ability to choose the projects that excite you most. But along with that freedom comes an often-overlooked responsibility—the need to manage your own benefits. This is a crucial step in building a stable, secure future for yourself, both during your working years and beyond.

We've already touched on the importance of setting up a strong retirement plan in the previous chapter, but your future security doesn't stop there. Freelancers also need to think about other important benefits like health insurance, dental and vision coverage, long-term care insurance, and even disability insurance. These are all essential pieces of the puzzle that will help you stay healthy, protected, and financially secure as you move forward in your career.

In this chapter, we'll dive into why it's critical for freelancers to create their own benefits package, share stories from freelancers who've successfully built theirs, and give you tips on finding the right mix of coverage for your needs.

Why Benefits Matter for Freelancers

In a traditional 9-to-5 job, employers typically handle most of the benefits: health insurance, dental coverage, retirement savings, and more. But as a freelancer, these responsibilities fall squarely on your shoulders. And that's a good thing—because it means you get to tailor a benefits package that fits your unique needs and lifestyle.

Without proper benefits in place, freelancers can find themselves in tricky situations. Health issues, unexpected injuries, or even the natural process of aging can turn into massive financial burdens. And let's face it, without the security of a well-rounded benefits plan, you might feel pressured to work long past the point you'd planned to retire, just to keep yourself financially afloat.

Building your own benefits package gives you control over your future, empowering you to safeguard your health, income, and quality of life. Plus, it helps create peace of mind so that you can focus on what matters most: growing your freelance business and living life on your terms.

Amanda's Journey: From Freelance Freedom to Full Coverage

Take Amanda, a freelance content writer based out of sunny California. She loved the freedom her freelance career offered, but after a few years, she realized she wasn't preparing for her future. She had no health insurance, no dental coverage, and certainly no retirement plan. "I was so focused on building my business that I forgot to build security for myself," Amanda admits.

Amanda decided to make a change. After some research, she found an ACA (Affordable Care Act) health plan that fit her budget, added dental and vision coverage, and set up a disability insurance policy. This simple shift made Amanda feel more secure in her freelance journey. Now she knows she's covered, no matter what life throws her way.

"I used to think benefits were only for people with traditional jobs," Amanda shared. "But now I realize that as a freelancer, I have the power to create my own plan—and that's a pretty powerful feeling."

Dave's Long-Term Vision: Securing His Health and Wealth

FINANCE FOR FREELANCERS

Then there's Dave, a freelance web designer from Chicago. After freelancing for 15 years, Dave began to think seriously about his long-term health. He knew that as he got older, medical expenses would likely increase. After all, freelancers don't get the luxury of an employer-sponsored benefits package, so he needed to plan carefully.

Dave connected with a healthcare broker to explore his options. He secured health insurance, added dental and vision coverage, and even invested in **long-term care insurance**—a smart move that would cover any future medical or assisted living needs as he aged. By thinking ahead and securing comprehensive coverage, Dave not only protected his health, but also his financial well-being.

"Planning ahead was the best thing I could have done for my peace of mind," said Dave. "Now I know that if something happens down the road, I won't be scrambling for coverage."

Ways to Build Your Own Benefits Package

So, how can you follow in Amanda and Dave's footsteps and build your own benefits package? It may sound overwhelming, but with the right approach, you can create a well-rounded plan that covers all the essentials. Here's how to get started:

1. **Health Insurance** Health insurance is the cornerstone of any benefits package. Whether you're young and healthy or have pre-existing conditions, medical costs can add up fast. The ACA Marketplace is a great starting point, but you can also explore private healthcare options or healthcare brokers who specialize in freelance plans.

2. **Dental and Vision Insurance** Dental and vision insurance are often overlooked, but they're just as important as health insurance. Routine check-ups, cleanings, and eye exams can prevent bigger, costlier issues down the road.

3. **Long-Term Care Insurance** Long-term care insurance covers services like in-home care, nursing home care, and assisted living facilities. It's a smart move to consider as you get older, helping you prepare for the unexpected.

4. **Disability Insurance** Freelancers depend entirely on their ability to work. If you were to get injured or sick, how would you pay your bills? Disability insur-

ance can provide a safety net by replacing a portion of your income if you can't work due to injury or illness.

5. **Find Local Help** Finding a healthcare broker or financial advisor in your area can be incredibly helpful. They'll help you sift through the overwhelming number of options and find plans that fit your specific needs. You can check online reviews or ask fellow freelancers for recommendations.

Companies to Explore for Freelance Benefits

When it comes to finding the right benefits package, you don't have to go it alone. Here are a few companies and resources that cater specifically to freelancers:

Freelancers Union: This nonprofit offers health insurance plans tailored to freelancers, as well as other resources like disability insurance and retirement savings options.

eHealthInsurance: An online marketplace that allows you to compare health, dental, and vision insurance plans from different providers, making it easier to find the best coverage for your needs.

Vanguard: Known for low-cost retirement investment options, Vanguard is a go-to for freelancers looking to set up SEP IRAs or Solo 401(k) plans.

Fidelity: Another popular option for freelancers, offering a wide range of retirement accounts, including Roth IRAs and Solo 401(k)s.

VSP and Guardian Insurance: These two companies provide low-cost vision and dental insurance packages that are perfect for freelancers.

Tips and Tricks for Building Your Benefits Package

1. **Start with Health Insurance**: This is the foundation of any benefits package. Once you've secured health insurance, you can build on that with other essential benefits like dental, vision, and disability insurance.

2. **Don't Overlook Long-Term Care Insurance**: This is especially important for freelancers nearing their 40s or older. Long-term care insurance can save you

from high medical bills later in life.

3. **Automate Your Contributions**: If you're contributing to a retirement plan or saving for healthcare expenses through an HSA, set up automatic transfers so you don't have to think about it. Even small, consistent contributions add up over time.

4. **Seek Professional Help**: A financial advisor or healthcare broker can help you navigate the sometimes-confusing world of freelance benefits. They'll ensure you're making the best decisions for your future.

Wrapping Up

Freelancing gives you the ultimate freedom, but with that freedom comes the responsibility of taking care of your own benefits. Don't wait until it's too late to think about health insurance, dental coverage, or retirement savings. Start building your benefits package today, and you'll be protecting not only your present self but also your future.

Whether you're just starting out or have been freelancing for years, creating a comprehensive benefits package will give you the peace of mind that comes from knowing you're covered—no matter what life throws your way. And remember, if you're feeling overwhelmed, don't hesitate to seek professional advice. Your future self will thank you for it!

Chapter 20: Keeping Debt in Check

"Interest on debts grows without rain." -Yiddish Proverb

Debt. Just saying the word makes your stomach tighten a bit, right? It's one of those topics nobody loves to talk about, but as freelancers, we have to face it head-on. Unlike a traditional 9-to-5, where a steady paycheck rolls in every two weeks, freelancing is a rollercoaster ride of income highs and lows. And guess what? Debt is not your friend on this wild ride. It's the weight that holds you down when you need to soar.

So, why is it so crucial to limit debt when you're a freelancer? Well, we'll dive into that, along with practical action steps to help you keep your debt manageable, and, of course, some tips and tricks to keep things fun and in control.

The Freelancer's Relationship with Debt

As a freelancer, you're your own boss (yay!), which also means you're your own financial planner, HR department, and accountant (yikes!). Debt can creep up on you fast—whether it's to pay for business expenses, invest in tools or courses, or manage personal finances when work slows down.

But here's the thing: Unlike employees with regular salaries, freelancers don't have the luxury of guaranteed income. This makes carrying debt especially risky. Imagine a slow month (or three), and you've got a hefty credit card balance hanging over your head. The interest piles up, the payments feel bigger, and suddenly, you're stressed out about money when you should be focused on getting your next gig.

Debt drains your energy. It siphons off the hard-earned money you could be saving for taxes, retirement, or reinvesting in your business. More importantly, it adds unnecessary stress to your already demanding freelance life. So, let's talk about how to keep it in check.

Why Limiting Debt Is So Important for Freelancers

Income Uncertainty: The first and most obvious reason to avoid debt is that your income fluctuates. Even the most successful freelancers experience ups and downs. Debt is dangerous because it assumes you'll always have enough money coming in to cover it. In reality, there will be months where you're swimming in cash, and others where you're wading in puddles.

Interest and Fees Pile Up: Credit cards, loans, and other forms of debt come with interest rates that can quickly spiral out of control. Before you know it, you're paying double what you originally borrowed, and that's money you could be putting into your business or savings instead.

It Limits Your Freedom: Remember, freelancing is all about freedom—financial freedom, time freedom, lifestyle freedom. Debt ties you down. It forces you to take on projects you might not love just because you need to pay off that looming balance.

Financial Stability: One of the best feelings in the world as a freelancer is knowing you're financially stable. Debt erodes that sense of security. It adds unpredictability to an already unpredictable career path. Limiting debt helps you maintain control and confidence in your financial future.

Peace of Mind: Less debt means less stress. It's that simple. You're already juggling clients, deadlines, and marketing your services. The last thing you need is the constant worry of mounting debt.

Action Steps to Start Limiting Your Debt

Now that we've established why keeping debt in check is so important, let's get into some actionable steps to help you start limiting debt today.

1. Create a Clear Budget

As a freelancer, your income fluctuates, so a traditional budget might not work for you. Instead, try a variable budget. Break down your monthly expenses into essential categories like rent, groceries, utilities, taxes, and debt payments. Once you have a clear picture of your monthly expenses, you can better manage what's coming in and what's going out.

2. Establish an Emergency Fund

We've talked about this before, but it bears repeating: An emergency fund is crucial for freelancers. Start by aiming for three to six months' worth of expenses. This fund will be your safety net for slow months, unexpected expenses, or taking time off without racking up debt.

3. Use Debt Wisely

Not all debt is bad. If you need to invest in something that will help grow your business, like equipment or a course, that's strategic debt. Just be smart about it. Make sure whatever you're spending on will lead to more income in the future, and don't borrow more than you can pay back quickly.

4. Pay More Than the Minimum

Paying the minimum on credit cards is a trap. Interest builds up, and you'll end up paying much more than the original amount. Whenever possible, pay more than the minimum balance to get ahead of the game.

5. Consolidate and Refinance

If you have multiple forms of debt, look into consolidating them into one loan with a lower interest rate. This can make managing payments easier and save you money on interest. Refinancing can also help lower interest rates and reduce monthly payments, freeing up cash flow for other needs.

6. Increase Your Rates

One of the best ways to get ahead of debt is to make more money! If you haven't raised your rates in a while, it might be time to do so. You deserve to be paid what you're worth, and boosting your income can help you stay on top of any debt more easily.

Tips and Tricks for Keeping Debt in Check

1. Use the 50/30/20 Rule

The 50/30/20 rule is a great guideline for managing your income. Allocate 50% of your earnings to needs (rent, utilities, groceries), 30% to wants (entertainment, dining out), and 20% to savings and debt repayment. Adjust the percentages based on your situation, but this is a solid framework to ensure you're living within your means and paying down debt.

2. Automate Payments

Set up automatic payments for your debt so you never miss a payment. If you can, automate extra payments toward your principal to pay off debt faster. Automating savings (when your income allows for it) can also keep you on track without having to think about it.

3. Stay Disciplined During Windfalls

Freelancing can come with unexpected income boosts—an extra big project, a client that pays more than expected, or a sudden rush of work. Instead of treating yourself to a shopping spree or a fancy vacation, put that extra cash toward paying down debt or building your emergency fund. Your future self will thank you.

4. Set Small, Achievable Goals

When you're deep in debt, the numbers can feel overwhelming. Break it down into smaller, manageable goals. Focus on paying off one credit card or loan at a time, starting with the smallest balance or the highest interest rate. Each time you hit a milestone, celebrate! It'll keep you motivated.

5. Track Your Progress

There's nothing more satisfying than seeing your debt shrink. Use an app or a simple spreadsheet to track your debt repayments. Watching those balances go down will inspire you to keep pushing forward, and it'll remind you that you're on the right path.

6. Cut Out Unnecessary Expenses

Take a good, hard look at where your money is going. Are there subscriptions you don't need? Can you cut back on dining out or impulse buys? Redirect that money to pay down debt faster. You'd be surprised how much you can save with a little discipline.

Wrapping It Up

Debt can feel like an intimidating monster lurking in the background, but as a freelancer, you have the power to tame it. By keeping a close eye on your expenses, building a budget that works for your unique income, and making smart, strategic choices when it comes to borrowing, you can keep debt in check and avoid unnecessary stress.

Remember, freelancing is all about freedom—don't let debt steal that freedom away. Be proactive, stay disciplined, and celebrate your wins along the way. With a little effort and determination, you can keep your finances healthy and your freelance business thriving. Let's get to work!

Chapter 21: Big Dreams, Bigger Purchases

> *"It is thrifty to prepare today for the wants of tomorrow."* -Aesop, Greek storyteller

Freelancing offers a lot of freedom. But with that freedom comes a unique set of financial responsibilities—especially when it comes to making big purchases. Whether it's upgrading your business equipment, splurging on a dream vacation, or investing in your future, big purchases can either be a major win for your lifestyle and career or a fast track to financial stress.

So, how do you navigate the world of big buys without derailing your finances? By saving smartly and deciding carefully. In this chapter, we'll dive into why it's important to save for big purchases, which ones to prioritize (whether they're freelance-related or personal), how to decide if a purchase is truly necessary, and some action steps to help you build up the funds before you swipe that card.

Why Saving for Big Purchases Matters

As freelancers, we don't have the luxury of a steady paycheck coming in every two weeks. Our income can be unpredictable, and that means big purchases—whether for business or personal reasons—need to be well-planned. The last thing you want is to find yourself deep in debt or tapping into your emergency fund because you didn't prepare for that fancy new laptop or a much-needed vacation.

Saving for big purchases allows you to:

Avoid Debt: Paying for something outright with saved funds means you won't have to rely on credit cards or loans that come with interest rates.

Plan Around Your Cash Flow: Instead of splurging when you're riding a wave of income and then panicking when it slows down, saving over time ensures you're not disrupting your financial balance.

Prevent Buyer's Remorse: Big purchases require careful consideration. Saving forces you to think long and hard about whether you really need something, helping to curb impulse buys that could hurt your finances.

Feel Empowered: There's something satisfying about saving for something and paying for it outright. You'll feel in control of your money and be more appreciative of what you buy.

Common Big Purchases for Freelancers and Beyond

Whether you're buying something to improve your business or for personal reasons, here are some common big purchases you might need to plan for:

Freelance-Related Purchases:

New Laptop or Computer: Your tools are everything in freelancing, especially if you're in a creative or tech field. But high-quality equipment comes with a hefty price tag.

Software Subscriptions: While monthly subscriptions might not seem like a big purchase at first, premium software for design, accounting, project management, or editing can add up quickly over time.

Business Courses or Certifications: Investing in your skills is essential for staying competitive, but professional courses or certifications can cost hundreds or even thousands of dollars.

Home Office Setup: From ergonomic chairs to a faster Wi-Fi connection or a high-end monitor, building a productive home office can require some serious cash.

Professional Photography Equipment: If you're a photographer or videographer, upgrading your camera, lenses, and gear can be one of the biggest expenses you'll face.

Marketing or Branding Services: Hiring a professional to help boost your personal brand or market your business is an investment in your future success, but it's not cheap.

<u>**Personal Purchases:**</u>

Vacation or Travel: Everyone needs a break, and freelancers aren't any different. However, without paid vacation time, planning for time away—and covering the cost of the trip itself—requires smart saving.

New Car: Whether for business or personal use, buying a car is a significant financial commitment.

Down Payment for a Home: Many freelancers dream of homeownership, but qualifying for a mortgage and saving for a down payment takes careful planning.

Medical Expenses: Health insurance can only cover so much. Sometimes you'll need to plan for out-of-pocket expenses for dental work, surgeries, or other health-related costs.

Is It Really Necessary? How to Decide if a Big Purchase is Worth It

Before you set your heart (and wallet) on a major buy, it's crucial to ask yourself whether it's truly necessary. Here are some questions to help guide you:

1. **Will This Purchase Improve My Business or Quality of Life?** If the answer is yes, then it might be worth it. For freelancers, investing in tools that improve productivity, quality, or efficiency is often a wise move. On the personal side, consider if this purchase will bring long-term happiness or solve an ongoing issue.

2. **Can I Afford This Right Now Without Dipping Into Emergency Funds?** If you can't afford it comfortably, it's time to start saving. Don't rush into a purchase if it's going to jeopardize your financial safety net.

3. **Is There a More Affordable Alternative?** Sometimes, there are less expensive ways to meet the same need. For example, can you lease equipment rather than buy it? Can you take a more budget-friendly vacation?

4. **Is This an Impulse Buy?** Take 24-48 hours to think it over before making any big purchase. If it still feels necessary after some time has passed, then it's worth considering. If not, you've likely saved yourself from buyer's remorse.

Action Steps for Saving for Big Purchases

Once you've determined that the purchase is necessary, it's time to start planning and saving.

1. Set a Target Amount

First, figure out exactly how much you need to save. Do some research on the cost of what you're planning to buy, including taxes, shipping, and any additional fees. Write this amount down and make it your target.

2. Break It Down Into Smaller Goals

Rather than trying to save the entire amount at once, break it down into monthly or weekly goals. If you need $2,000 for a new computer and want to buy it in six months, set a goal to save around $334 each month. Breaking it down into smaller chunks makes it more manageable.

3. Create a Separate Savings Account

One of the best ways to stay on track is to create a dedicated savings account for your big purchase. This keeps the money separate from your daily expenses and helps you track your progress. Some banks even let you create "buckets" within your savings account for different goals.

4. Automate Your Savings

If your income is fairly stable, consider automating your savings by setting up a monthly transfer into your savings account. This way, you don't have to think about it, and the money is saved before you can spend it on something else.

5. Cut Back on Non-Essentials

If you're serious about making a big purchase, look for areas in your budget where you can cut back temporarily. Maybe skip a few dinners out or cut down on streaming services for a while. Small sacrifices can add up quickly.

Stories of Freelancers Who Saved for Big Purchases

Let's take a look at a couple of freelance success stories to inspire you:

Casey's New Camera Equipment

Casey is a freelance photographer who's been working with the same camera for years. It's served him well, but as his business grew, he knew he needed to upgrade to more professional equipment to attract higher-paying clients. Instead of putting the camera on his credit card, he decided to start a savings plan. He set aside a portion of his income from each gig and made small sacrifices—like cutting back on eating out and buying second-hand clothes. After eight months, he had saved enough to buy the new equipment outright. The best part? The new camera paid for itself within two months by landing him a major wedding photography gig.

Sarah's Dream Vacation

Sarah is a freelance writer who's been dreaming of a trip to Bali. However, without the security of paid vacation days, taking time off and affording the trip seemed impossible. Sarah created a vacation fund, setting aside 10% of her income each month. She also started picking up extra work during her busier months to fast-track her savings. After a year of dedicated saving, she had enough to cover the cost of the trip and her living expenses for the month off. She returned to work recharged and ready to tackle new clients.

Tips and Tricks for Saving for Big Purchases

1. Use Windfalls Wisely

Whenever you receive unexpected money—whether from a big client project, a tax refund, or a gift—direct a portion of it toward your savings goal.

2. Sell What You Don't Use

If you're upgrading equipment, try selling your old gear to help fund the new purchase. The same goes for personal items—selling unused furniture, clothes, or electronics can give your savings a boost.

3. Reward Yourself for Milestones

Saving for a big purchase can take time, so keep yourself motivated by celebrating small wins along the way. When you reach a savings milestone, treat yourself to something small—just don't dip into your savings to do it!

4. Track Your Progress

Use a budgeting app or a simple spreadsheet to track your savings progress. Seeing how far you've come can give you the encouragement you need to keep going.

5. Be Patient and Persistent

Saving for a big purchase takes time, especially when you're a freelancer juggling unpredictable income. Stay patient, and don't rush the process. Remember that saving over time means you'll enjoy your purchase even more when you finally get it.

Wrapping It Up

Big purchases, whether for business or pleasure, are part of the freelancing journey. They're exciting milestones that can either propel your business forward or add joy to your life—if you approach them wisely. The key is to plan, save diligently, and avoid unnecessary debt. By following the action steps and tips in this chapter, you'll be better equipped to make those big buys while keeping your finances on solid ground.

Happy saving, and here's to smart spending!

Chapter 22: Investing in Your Success

"You can only become truly accomplished at something you love. Don't make money your goal. Instead, pursue the things you love doing, and then do them so well that people can't take their eyes off you." -Maya Angelou

As freelancers, we often wear multiple hats—marketer, accountant, customer service rep, content creator, and more. It's easy to get caught up in the day-to-day grind and forget that, like any business, our freelance ventures need a solid investment strategy to grow and thrive.

Investing in your freelance business isn't just about throwing money at problems. It's about making strategic choices that increase your skills, improve your efficiency, attract more clients, and ultimately boost your income. Whether you're putting in time, money, or energy, smart investments can turn your freelance hustle into a full-blown, profitable business.

In this chapter, we'll dive into why investing in your freelance business is crucial, explore the different kinds of investments you can make, and share some stories of freelancers who've taken the leap and reaped the rewards. Plus, I'll give you some actionable tips and tricks to help you start investing in your own success today.

Why Investing in Your Freelance Business is a Game-Changer

Imagine trying to grow a garden without ever planting new seeds or adding water. Sure, you might get some flowers from time to time, but without regular care and investment, that garden won't thrive. The same goes for your freelance business. If you're not continuously putting effort, time, and resources into your business, it's going to stay stagnant—or worse, wither away.

When you invest in your business, you're sending a powerful message to yourself (and your clients) that you're serious about your craft. Here are a few reasons why investing is crucial:

It Keeps You Competitive

Freelancing is a competitive world. New tools, technologies, and trends are always emerging. If you're not keeping up by investing in your skills or upgrading your tools, you risk falling behind. Clients want to work with freelancers who are on the cutting edge of their field, and that requires ongoing investment.

It Boosts Your Confidence

When you invest in yourself and your business, it's like giving yourself a confidence injection. Whether it's a new laptop, a professional website, or taking an online course to level up your skills, these investments make you feel more equipped to tackle bigger and better projects. And that confidence? It shows in your work and in how you present yourself to clients.

It Leads to Growth

You can't grow your business if you're not willing to invest in it. Investing in marketing, for example, can attract higher-paying clients. Upgrading your equipment can help you deliver work more efficiently, freeing up time to take on more clients. Growth requires input—whether that's money, time, or energy.

It Future-Proofs Your Business

The freelance landscape is constantly evolving. By investing in your business, you're future-proofing yourself against changes in the market. Whether it's learning new skills or diversifying your income streams, these investments help you stay relevant and adaptable.

What Does Investing in Your Freelance Business Really Mean?

When most people hear the word "investing," they automatically think of money. While financial investment is a big part of it, investing in your freelance business comes in many forms. It's about putting in time, energy, and resources that will lead to long-term growth and success. Let's break it down.

Financial Investment

This is the most obvious type of investment, and yes, sometimes you'll need to spend money to make money. But financial investment doesn't have to mean draining your bank account. It's about spending smartly and strategically. Think of it as planting seeds that will yield a future harvest.

Some ways to financially invest in your business include:

- **Upgrading Your Equipment**: That old laptop that takes 10 minutes to boot up? It's holding you back. Investing in high-quality tools, like a fast computer, a professional camera, or top-notch design software, can help you work more efficiently and deliver better results.

- **Hiring Help**: Sometimes, the best investment you can make is in other people. If your time is better spent working with clients than handling administrative tasks, hire a virtual assistant. Need help with branding? Hire a designer. Don't be afraid to delegate.

- **Marketing and Advertising**: Whether it's running Facebook ads, investing in SEO for your website, or paying for a professional headshot, spending money on marketing can attract more clients and higher-paying projects.

Time Investment

Not all investments require money. Sometimes, the best thing you can invest is your time. Freelancers often fall into the trap of focusing solely on client work, leaving little time for their own business development. But carving out time to improve your business will pay off in the long run.

Ways to invest your time:

- **Learning New Skills**: Set aside time each week to learn something new that can benefit your business. This could be anything from mastering a new software program to taking a course in project management.

- **Networking**: Building relationships with other freelancers, industry professionals, and potential clients can open doors to new opportunities. Attending events, participating in online communities, and even grabbing coffee with a fellow freelancer are all great ways to invest in networking.

- **Building Your Portfolio**: Don't wait for the perfect client project to showcase your skills. Invest time in building a portfolio that highlights your best work. Create mock projects if necessary. A strong portfolio is one of your most powerful marketing tools.

Energy and Effort Investment

Freelancing requires hustle. You've got to be willing to put in the energy and effort to grow your business. This could mean staying up late to finish a project, spending extra time perfecting a proposal, or going the extra mile to deliver exceptional results for a client.

Some examples of energy investment include:

- **Client Relationships**: Building strong relationships with your clients takes effort, but it's one of the best investments you can make. Happy clients lead to repeat business, referrals, and long-term success.

- **Creating Systems**: Streamlining your business processes might not sound glamorous, but it can save you a ton of time and headaches down the road. Invest the energy now to set up efficient systems for tracking invoices, managing projects, and staying organized.

Stories of Freelancers Who Invested in Their Success

Laura's Leap into Design

Laura was a freelance graphic designer struggling to land high-paying clients. She realized her equipment and software were outdated, and it was holding her back. She decided to invest in a powerful new computer, the latest design software, and even took a specialized online course in UI/UX design. The upfront cost was a bit daunting, but the results were almost immediate. With her new tools and skills, she was able to attract bigger clients, offer more services, and raise her rates. Within six months, she had more than tripled her income.

Marcus' Marketing Magic

Marcus was a freelance writer with a solid client base, but he wanted to expand his business. He decided to invest in marketing by hiring a professional to redesign his website and paying for SEO services. He also invested in Facebook ads to reach new clients. The marketing paid off—within three months, his website traffic doubled, and he started landing higher-paying projects from clients who found him online. His initial investment in marketing quickly paid for itself, and his business has been growing ever since.

How You Can Start Investing in Your Freelance Business

You don't have to invest everything all at once. In fact, it's better to start small and focus on the areas where investment will have the biggest impact on your business. Here are some action steps to get you started:

Identify Your Business Needs

Take a step back and assess where your business could use a boost. Do you need better tools or equipment? Are you lacking in a certain skill area? Do you need more clients? Once you've identified your needs, you can start thinking about where to invest.

Set a Budget

Whether you're investing time or money, it's important to set a budget. How much time can you realistically devote to learning a new skill each week? How much money can you set aside for business expenses? Setting a budget ensures that you're investing wisely and not overextending yourself.

Start Small

You don't need to make huge investments right away. Start small by upgrading one piece of equipment or taking one online course. As your business grows, you can reinvest your profits into more significant improvements.

Track Your ROI

It's important to track the return on your investment (ROI) to make sure your investments are paying off. Are you landing more clients after investing in marketing? Is your workflow more efficient after upgrading your tools? Regularly evaluate the impact of your investments to ensure you're getting the most bang for your buck.

Tips and Tricks for Smart Freelance Investing

1. **Reinvest Your Profits**: As your business grows and you start earning more, reinvest a portion of your profits into further business development.

2. **Take Advantage of Free Resources**: Not every investment requires money. There are countless free courses, webinars, and tools available online that can help you level up your skills without breaking the bank.

3. **Join a Freelance Community**: Surrounding yourself with like-minded freelancers can be an invaluable investment. Freelance communities often offer resources, job leads, and networking opportunities.

4. **Focus on High-Impact Areas**: Invest in the areas that will have the biggest impact on your business. For example, if you're a freelance photographer, investing in a high-quality camera will likely yield a better ROI than spending money on fancy business cards.

Final Thoughts

Investing in your freelance business is one of the smartest decisions you can make. Whether it's time, money, or energy, the investments you make today will pay off in the form of more clients, better projects, and higher earnings down the road. Remember, you're not just a freelancer—you're the CEO of your business. And every CEO knows that success comes from investing in growth.

Now go out there and start investing in your future!

Chapter 23: Profit Tune-Up: How to Keep Your Rates Aligned With Your Value

"If you don't value your time, neither will others. Stop giving away your time and talents. Value what you know and start charging for it." -Kim Garst, marketing strategist

In the fast-paced world of freelancing, your pricing structure can make or break your business. The rates you set directly impact how much you earn, the quality of clients you attract, and even how you're perceived in your industry. Pricing is not a one-and-done decision; it's something that needs to be revisited regularly. As markets evolve, so do the expectations and budgets of your clients, meaning you need to stay nimble and adaptable to ensure you're getting paid what you're worth. In this chapter, we'll explore why it's essential to evaluate your pricing regularly, how to approach the process, and share practical examples of freelancers who did it right.

Why Regularly Evaluating Pricing is Crucial

The freelancing world is not static. What worked when you started out might not hold up as you gain more experience, expand your portfolio, or as industry standards shift. Regularly reviewing your pricing helps you:

Stay Competitive: Freelance markets can be flooded with talent, and your rates must reflect your value while staying competitive. Undervaluing yourself may attract lower-quality clients who don't appreciate your skills, while overpricing can drive potential clients away.

Account for Inflation and Rising Costs: The cost of living and doing business changes every year. If you're charging the same rate you did five years ago, you're probably losing money in real terms. Adjusting for inflation ensures your earnings match the reality of your expenses.

Reflect Your Growth: As you gain more experience and expertise, your skills are worth more. Regularly evaluating your pricing allows you to charge for the added value you bring to clients based on your increased proficiency.

Avoid Burnout: Setting prices too low might mean you're working more hours just to break even. Evaluating your pricing helps ensure you're not overworking yourself for less than you're worth.

Adapt to Market Changes: Industries change, as do client budgets and expectations. Keeping a pulse on your market allows you to adjust your pricing based on current demand.

How to Evaluate Your Pricing

The process of evaluating your pricing can seem daunting, but it doesn't have to be. By following these steps, you can regularly assess your rates and make adjustments where necessary.

Analyze Your Current Client Base: Start by reviewing the clients you currently have. Are they paying your desired rates? If not, it might be time to reassess how much you're charging. Look at which clients are your highest earners and which ones might be paying less than they should.

Assess the Value You Provide: Evaluate what you bring to the table for your clients. Do you offer a unique skill set or service that few others do? Have you improved your speed or the quality of your work since your last price adjustment? Be honest with yourself—your rates should reflect the true value you deliver.

Research Industry Standards: It's essential to know what others in your field are charging. Use online freelance rate calculators, industry-specific surveys, and networking with peers to gather this information. Websites like Upwork, Freelancers Union, and PayScale often publish up-to-date information about average rates for various freelance roles.

Account for Expenses and Taxes: Many freelancers forget to factor in the true cost of doing business when they set their rates. Be sure to include your overhead (software, tools, office space, etc.) and taxes when determining what you should be charging.

Survey the Market: Keep an eye on changes in your industry. Are more freelancers entering the field? Are new technologies reducing the time it takes to complete certain tasks? Stay informed about industry trends and how they impact pricing.

Resources for Evaluating Your Pricing

Here are some tools and resources to help you regularly assess and adjust your rates:

Freelance Rate Calculators: Websites like **Freelance Switch** and **YourRate.co** offer simple calculators that factor in your costs and desired income to help you set appropriate rates.

Salary Surveys: Websites like **Glassdoor**, **PayScale**, and **Indeed** publish salary surveys that can provide insights into what others in your field are making. This is especially useful for comparing rates across different geographic locations or levels of experience.

Freelancers Union: This organization regularly releases reports on freelancer earnings, industry trends, and common pricing structures.

Upwork and Fiverr: If you're on platforms like these, you can search for freelancers offering similar services to see what rates they're charging.

Networking Groups: Join freelance communities on social media or platforms like **LinkedIn**. You can often gather information about pricing trends from your peers.

Stories of Freelancers Who Benefited from Regular Pricing Reviews

Case 1: The Web Designer Who Doubled Her Income

Megan, a freelance web designer, had been charging the same rates for three years. She was always busy, but no matter how many projects she took on, she never seemed to have enough money saved. After sitting down to analyze her rates, Megan realized she wasn't factoring in her software subscriptions or the added value of her experience. She increased her rates by 30%, and though she initially feared losing clients, none of them blinked an eye. In fact, she landed a new client who was happy to pay her higher rates because of her expertise. Within six months, Megan doubled her income without taking on any more clients than before.

Case 2: The Copywriter Who Found His Niche

Ben, a freelance copywriter, struggled to find clients who were willing to pay his rates. After researching industry standards and surveying his client base, Ben realized that the broad range of services he was offering—blog writing, website content, social media posts—was undervaluing his skills. He decided to focus on high-conversion email copywriting, a niche he was passionate about, and increased his rates to reflect the specialized nature of his services. Within a year, Ben was working with fewer clients but making more money than ever before.

Case 3: The Graphic Designer Who Avoided Burnout

Linda, a graphic designer, was constantly overworked, handling a multitude of small projects that paid little but required a lot of time and effort. After evaluating her pricing structure, Linda realized she needed to charge more for her time-intensive projects. She also decided to implement package pricing, which bundled her services and provided better value for clients while allowing her to earn more in fewer hours. This change not only prevented burnout but gave her more free time to focus on creative projects she loved.

Action Steps: How to Implement a Pricing Review

Block Off Time: Dedicate time in your calendar to thoroughly review your current pricing. Aim to do this every quarter or twice a year.

Gather Data: Collect relevant information, such as industry standards, client feedback, and your current financial situation, to inform your pricing decisions.

Test the Waters: Before raising your rates across the board, try adjusting them with new clients first. If the change is well-received, apply it to existing clients.

Update Your Contracts: Ensure your contracts and agreements reflect your new pricing and any adjustments you've made.

Stay Informed: Join freelancing communities and subscribe to industry reports to stay updated on market trends and changes that might influence your pricing.

Tips and Tricks for Regular Pricing Evaluations

1. **Set a Schedule**: Don't leave price evaluations to chance. Set a specific time each quarter or biannually to sit down and review your rates. Mark it on your calendar to ensure it gets done.

2. **Start Small**: If the idea of raising your rates is intimidating, try increasing them gradually. You don't have to jump 30% overnight. A 5-10% increase can still make a noticeable difference in your income over time.

3. **Communicate with Clients**: When raising rates, be sure to communicate the value you're offering to your clients. Most clients won't mind paying more if they see a clear benefit, such as faster turnaround times or improved service quality.

4. **Create Tiered Pricing**: Offering different pricing tiers allows you to appeal to a broader range of clients. For example, a basic package might include fewer services at a lower rate, while premium packages can offer more features at a higher price.

5. **Consider Retainer Agreements**: A retainer agreement is a great way to ensure

steady income from clients who need ongoing work. While these may initially come at a slightly lower rate, the consistency and reliability can be worth it in the long run.

By regularly evaluating your pricing, you ensure that your freelance business not only survives but thrives. Staying flexible and adaptive will help you grow, avoid burnout, and maintain a high-quality client base willing to pay what you're worth.

Chapter 24: Keeping the Momentum Going

"***M***oney *grows on the tree of persistence.*" -Japanese proverb

Your freelance business is a living, breathing entity that requires attention, nurturing, and most importantly—regular checkups. While it's easy to focus on the daily grind, the bigger picture is just as crucial. Sure, we talked about evaluating pricing in the last chapter (because money matters!), but there's so much more to running a successful freelance business.

In this chapter, we'll explore the importance of reviewing *everything* in your freelance business regularly—your services, clients, branding, and even your preferred type of client. Think of it as your business' personal tune-up, keeping everything running smoothly and efficiently. By doing this, you not only stay ahead of the curve but also make adjustments before problems arise.

Why Reviewing Your Freelance Business Regularly is Essential

Freelancing is a dynamic field, where things change fast—your skills, the market, and your clients' needs. Without regular check-ins, you might find yourself offering services that no longer light you up or catering to clients who aren't aligned with your vision. The beauty of freelancing is the ability to pivot quickly, and regular reviews give you the insights you need to stay adaptable and thrive.

Here are a few key reasons to make business reviews a habit:

Stay Aligned with Your Goals: As your business grows, so do your personal and professional goals. Regular reviews ensure that your freelance business is still aligned with where you want to go.

Enhance Efficiency: Regularly auditing how you work, the tools you use, and the clients you serve helps you streamline processes and improve productivity.

Boost Satisfaction: Freelancing should bring you joy! By reassessing your services and clients, you can steer your business toward projects that excite you and weed out the ones that don't.

Evolve Your Brand: Your brand is the heart of your business. It represents who you are and what you stand for. As you evolve, so should your brand, and regular reviews help you stay authentic.

Things to Review in Your Freelance Business

Let's dive into the specific areas of your freelance business that deserve a regular review. Think of this as your ultimate checklist, a toolkit for ensuring your business stays on track and true to your vision.

Services Offered

Are the services you're offering still the ones you want to offer? It's easy to get caught in the routine of providing the same services, but as you grow, your expertise changes, and so does the market. Maybe there's a new skill you've acquired that you're eager to offer or perhaps a service that's no longer in demand.

Example: Sarah, a graphic designer, started her freelance career designing logos. Over time, she discovered a passion for brand strategy and started offering that as a service. After her last business review, she realized that brand strategy was not only more fulfilling but also more lucrative. She decided to phase out logo design and focus on strategy, positioning herself as an expert in the field.

Action Step: Make a list of the services you currently offer. Next, list the services you *want* to offer. Are there any services you should phase out? Is there something new you want to introduce to attract different clients or work on more fulfilling projects?

Current Clients

Your clients play a massive role in your business' success and happiness. Some clients might have been a great fit when you started working with them, but as your skills and business have evolved, they might not be the best match anymore.

Take some time to assess your current client roster:

- **Do they pay on time?**
- **Do they value your work and respect your time?**
- **Are they helping you reach your financial goals?**
- **Do you enjoy working with them?**

Example: Jason, a freelance content writer, had a mix of clients when he started, from small businesses to major corporations. After conducting a review, he noticed that his smaller clients required more hand-holding and were often late with payments. He decided to focus solely on corporate clients, where the pay was higher, and processes were smoother.

Action Step: Evaluate your current clients against your business goals. Which ones are a joy to work with? Which ones drain your energy or cause unnecessary stress? It's okay to let go of clients who no longer align with your vision. Create an "ideal client profile" and use that to guide your decisions going forward.

Branding

Your brand is more than your logo or website—it's how you communicate your values, your personality, and the unique value you bring to clients. As you grow, it's essential that your branding grows with you.

Ask yourself:

- **Is my website reflective of my current services and skill level?**
- **Does my social media presence align with my brand values?**
- **Are my branding materials (logo, colors, fonts, etc.) consistent and mod-**

ern?

Example: Lena, a freelance digital marketer, started out targeting small startups with her branding. But as her expertise grew, she began working with larger companies. When she reviewed her branding, she realized her website and marketing materials were outdated and didn't reflect her new clientele. She rebranded to attract more high-paying, established businesses.

Action Step: Audit your branding materials—your website, social media profiles, logo, and tagline. Do they accurately reflect who you are today? If not, it might be time for a refresh!

Preferred Clients

Not all clients are created equal. Some will align with your vision, respect your work, and make your business a joy to run. Others, not so much. Part of the beauty of freelancing is the ability to choose who you work with. But sometimes, we forget that we have the power to say "no" or to actively pursue the clients we *want* to work with.

Example: Karen, a freelance social media manager, realized during her last business review that her favorite projects involved working with non-profits. She made the decision to focus on attracting more non-profit clients, adjusting her marketing and outreach strategies to align with their needs.

Action Step: Identify your preferred clients. Are they in a specific industry? Do they have a certain budget? Are they located in a specific region? Once you know who they are, think about how you can position yourself to attract them more effectively.

Action Steps to Implement a Regular Review

Here are some actionable steps to guide you through the process of regularly reviewing your business:

Schedule a Review Date: The first step is simply committing to the process. Choose a time once a quarter (or at least twice a year) to sit down and audit your freelance business.

Create a Review Checklist: Use the points above as a guide. Go through each aspect of your business systematically, from services to clients, branding, and more.

Set New Goals: Once you've reviewed the different aspects of your business, set new goals. These could include phasing out old services, launching new ones, updating your website, or targeting a different type of client.

Implement Changes Gradually: You don't have to overhaul everything at once. Make a plan to implement changes one step at a time. For example, if you're updating your website, start with your portfolio or client testimonials.

Tips and Tricks for Regular Business Reviews

1. **Use Feedback as a Tool**: Client feedback can offer valuable insights. Are you getting recurring comments about certain services or requests for new ones? Use this feedback to guide your business adjustments.

2. **Track Your Time**: During your review, look at how you're spending your time. Are you spending hours on administrative tasks? Could you outsource or automate these? A time-tracking tool like Toggl can help you see where your hours are going and where you can improve.

3. **Review Financials Regularly**: Make sure to look at your earnings, expenses, and cash flow. Are you meeting your financial goals? Are there areas where you could save money or increase income?

4. **Update Your Contracts**: When reviewing your services and pricing, don't forget to update your contracts. This ensures everything reflects your current offerings and protects you legally.

Conclusion

Running a successful freelance business isn't just about doing the work; it's about maintaining the business behind the work. Regularly reviewing your services, clients, branding, and preferred clients is essential for keeping your freelance career fulfilling, profitable, and aligned with your goals. The more intentional you are about these reviews, the more smoothly your business will run, and the more freedom you'll have to pursue projects that light you up.

By taking time to reflect and adjust, you'll ensure that your business not only stays afloat but thrives.

Chapter 25: Smart Financial Tools for Freelancers

"Wealth is largely the result of habit." -John Jacob Astor

Managing finances can often feel like one of the most overwhelming parts of freelancing. You're not just responsible for doing the work—you also need to track your income, handle expenses, issue invoices, and keep up with taxes. But the good news is that you don't have to do it alone. There's a wide array of financial software designed to help freelancers stay on top of their finances, often at little to no cost.

This chapter will introduce you to some of the best financial tools available for freelancers today, with a focus on affordable options. We'll also break down what each tool is used for, how it can streamline your business, and the steps you can take to get started.

Why Financial Software is a Game-Changer

Financial software can be a lifesaver for freelancers. Not only does it help you stay organized, but it can also save time, reduce stress, and ensure that you're fully prepared when tax season rolls around. By automating tasks like invoicing, tracking expenses, and budgeting, you free up more time to focus on what you do best—your freelance work.

Here are a few reasons why using financial software is essential:

Improved Organization: Financial software helps you keep all your financial information in one place, making it easy to find what you need quickly.

Time Savings: Automation features like recurring invoices and expense categorization save you countless hours of manual data entry.

Increased Accuracy: With built-in calculators and financial templates, these tools can help you avoid errors that might cost you later on.

Peace of Mind: With financial software, you know that your numbers are accurate, your invoices are sent on time, and your expenses are being tracked—all with minimal effort.

Types of Financial Software for Freelancers

Now that you know the importance of financial tools, let's dive into some of the best low-cost or free options available. This list covers a range of needs, from invoicing to budgeting to tax preparation.

Wave – Invoicing and Accounting (Free)

Wave is one of the best free financial tools available to freelancers. It offers a full suite of accounting features, including invoicing, expense tracking, and even payroll services if needed (although the payroll feature has a fee). Wave's easy-to-use interface and powerful features make it a popular choice for freelancers who need a full accounting solution without the hefty price tag.

- **What It's Used For**: Invoicing, income and expense tracking, and basic accounting.

- **Key Features**: Customizable invoices, recurring billing, and automatic expense categorization.

Action Step: Set up an account with Wave and create your first invoice. Try automating your recurring invoices and set up your bank feed to track expenses effortlessly.

QuickBooks Self-Employed – Tax Prep and Mileage Tracking (Low-Cost)

QuickBooks Self-Employed is another fantastic option for freelancers, especially those who want to be well-prepared for tax season. QuickBooks offers features like automatic mileage tracking, quarterly tax estimates, and seamless integration with TurboTax for easy tax filing.

- **What It's Used For**: Tracking expenses, calculating quarterly taxes, invoicing, and preparing for tax season.
- **Key Features**: Automatic tax calculations, mileage tracking, and the ability to separate business from personal expenses.

Action Step: Use QuickBooks' mileage tracking feature on your phone. This will automatically log your trips and calculate deductions based on business miles driven.

Zoho Invoice – Professional Invoicing (Free)

Zoho Invoice is another free tool that's excellent for freelancers who need simple but professional invoicing. You can customize invoices, set up automatic reminders, and even accept online payments through platforms like PayPal. Zoho also offers time tracking features for freelancers who charge by the hour.

- **What It's Used For**: Sending professional invoices, tracking time, and accepting payments.
- **Key Features**: Invoice templates, payment reminders, and time-tracking integration.

Action Step: Sign up for Zoho Invoice and create a custom invoice template for your freelance business. Set up automatic payment reminders for any clients with outstanding balances.

FreshBooks – All-in-One Invoicing and Accounting (Low-Cost)

FreshBooks is designed specifically with freelancers in mind, offering a user-friendly platform for invoicing, tracking expenses, and managing projects. Although not free, FreshBooks offers a low-cost option with pricing tiers based on how many clients you have. The software integrates with over 100 apps, making it easy to streamline your workflow.

- **What It's Used For**: Invoicing, expense tracking, project management, and financial reporting.
- **Key Features**: Time tracking, client collaboration tools, and payment acceptance.

Action Step: Try FreshBooks' time tracking tool to ensure you're billing clients accurately for the time you spend on their projects. Use its project management feature to keep all client communications in one place.

Toggl – Time Tracking (Free and Paid Plans)

Time is money, especially in the freelance world. Toggl is a fantastic tool for tracking your time, which is especially important if you bill clients by the hour. Even if you charge per project, Toggl helps you better understand how long tasks take so you can price your services more accurately in the future.

- **What It's Used For**: Tracking billable hours and improving time management.
- **Key Features**: One-click time tracking, detailed reports, and project time allocation.

Action Step: Start using Toggl to track the time you spend on different tasks. This will help you understand where your time goes, and you can use that data to adjust your rates or improve your workflow.

Rocket Money – Personal Finance and Budgeting (Low-Cost)

Rocket Money is a budgeting tool that does the basics well. It's easy to track your spending and set up budgets as well as create rules for automatically categorizing transactions. It has a free option as well as a premium option that is only $4 a month, paid annually, so perfect for freelancers.

- **What It's Used For**: Budgeting, tracking personal spending, and setting financial goals.
- **Key Features**: Budgeting tools, bill reminders, and credit score monitoring.

Action Step: Use Rocket Money to create a personal budget based on your freelance income. Set financial goals, such as saving for taxes or building an emergency fund.

PayPal – Online Payments (Low-Cost)

Most freelancers are familiar with PayPal as a way to receive payments, but did you know it also offers invoicing and expense tracking features? PayPal allows you to send professional invoices, track payments, and even link your PayPal account to other financial software.

- **What It's Used For**: Receiving payments, sending invoices, and tracking expenses.
- **Key Features**: Online payments, international transactions, and invoicing.

Action Step: Set up a PayPal account and link it to your other financial software, like QuickBooks or Wave, to track all your payments in one place.

Expensify – Expense Tracking (Free and Paid Plans)

Expensify is a handy tool for freelancers who need to track expenses, especially if you travel for work or purchase a lot of business-related items. You can scan receipts, categorize expenses, and generate reports for tax time.

- **What It's Used For**: Tracking expenses, scanning receipts, and generating expense reports.
- **Key Features**: Receipt scanning, mileage tracking, and expense categorization.

Action Step: Use Expensify to start scanning and categorizing your receipts. This will save you hours when tax season comes around, and you need to deduct business expenses.

Action Items to Get Started

Now that you have a list of financial tools at your fingertips, here's how to put them to use:

Choose Your Software: Start by selecting one or two tools that fit your current needs. If you're looking for invoicing and accounting, Wave or Zoho Invoice is a great place to start. If you need to track your time, Toggl is a fantastic option.

Automate Where Possible: Take advantage of automation features like recurring invoices, automatic mileage tracking, and payment reminders. These small time-savers will make a massive difference in your day-to-day operations.

Set Up a System: Financial tools are only helpful if you use them regularly. Set up a system for yourself where you check in on your finances weekly or monthly to ensure everything is running smoothly.

Track Your Time: Use time-tracking software to understand how long projects take and whether your current rates accurately reflect the time spent.

Stay Consistent: Consistency is key. Make it a habit to use your financial tools regularly so you can stay on top of your freelance finances, instead of scrambling during tax season.

Tips and Tricks for Maximizing Financial Software

1. **Start Simple**: If you're new to financial tools, don't overwhelm yourself by trying to use everything at once. Start with the basics—like invoicing and expense tracking—and gradually add in more features.

2. **Use Free Trials**: Most paid software options offer free trials, so take advantage of them! Test out a few different tools to see which ones best suit your workflow.

3. **Keep Personal and Business Finances Separate**: While tools like Mint can help you with personal finance, be sure to keep your business finances in a separate account. This makes tracking easier and helps you avoid tax headaches later.

4. **Sync with Your Bank**: Most financial software allows you to link your bank account, automatically pulling in transactions. This saves time and ensures

Conclusion

Incorporating financial software into your freelance business can be a game-changer. Not only do these tools help you stay organized and efficient, but they also free up time for you to focus on doing the work you love. Whether you're just getting started or are a seasoned freelancer, there's a software solution out there to help manage your invoicing, expenses, and even taxes—often at little to no cost.

By taking advantage of the powerful features these platforms offer, you can simplify your financial processes, reduce stress, and keep your business running smoothly. So, start exploring the options today, automate where you can, and watch how these tools can help you transform your freelance business from surviving to thriving.

Now it's your turn to take action—choose your software, set up your systems, and start maximizing your freelance potential!

CONCLUSION

*"**S**uccess is not the key to happiness. Happiness is the key to success. If you love what you are doing, you will be successful."* -Albert Schweitzer

As we come to the conclusion of *Finance for Freelancers: Maximize Income, Manage Cash Flow, Minimize Stress*, I want to congratulate you for taking the time to invest in yourself and your freelance business. Whether you're just starting out or you've been at it for a while, the fact that you're here, reading this, means you're committed to your growth and success as a freelancer. And that's something to be proud of.

Freelancing can be an incredibly rewarding journey, but as we've discussed, it comes with its own unique set of challenges—especially when it comes to managing your finances. It's easy to feel overwhelmed or lost in the shuffle, but my hope is that this book has provided you with the clarity, tools, and strategies you need to not only survive but truly thrive in your freelance business.

But this isn't the end of your journey—it's just the beginning. Financial success as a freelancer isn't about mastering a single concept or strategy; it's about continually evaluating and evolving, adjusting your goals as your business grows, and staying adaptable in an ever-changing market. The tools you've learned here are meant to grow with you, and as your freelance business develops, so too will your ability to maximize your income, manage your cash flow, and keep stress at bay.

For more guidance on creating and achieving the goals that will take your freelance business to the next level, I encourage you to check out my book *Dream Catchers: Mastering the Art of Realizing Your Dreams*. It's filled with inspiration and strategies for turning your dreams into actionable goals, something every freelancer needs in their toolkit. And if you're looking for even more freelance-specific strategies, I recommend my book *Freelance Success Secrets: 21 Essential Habits That Will Transform Your Freelance Business from Surviving to Thriving*. It dives deep into habits that will help you not just maintain your business, but elevate it to new heights.

I also want to extend a personal invitation for you to connect with me and a supportive community of freelancers in my private Facebook group, *The Freelancer's Life*. You can join us here: https://www.facebook.com/groups/thefreelancerslife . It's a space where we share tips, offer support, and celebrate our wins together. And don't forget to check out the Facebook page dedicated to freelancers here: https://www.facebook.com/thefreelancerslife. I'd love to see you there and continue this conversation as you grow your business.

In closing, I hope this book has provided you with the inspiration, motivation, resources, and tools you need to take your freelance business from just surviving to absolutely thriving. You have the power to create the life you want, and with the right financial strategies, you can free yourself from stress and focus on doing the work you love.

The freelance life is full of possibilities—embrace them, stay determined, and remember, the sky's the limit. You've got this!

PLEASE DO ME A HUGE FAVOR

Please do me a huge favor, if you have been inspired by my books and want to help others reach their freelance goals and improve their businesses too, here are some action steps you can take immediately to make a positive difference:

Write a review on Amazon for this book. Reviews are critical for authors, helping us sell more books and deliver more value to our readers. It also helps people looking for my books find them more easily. People are more apt to buy a book like this if there are positive reviews telling them how the book has helped its readers personally.

Gift my books. Gift my books to friends, family, colleagues, and even strangers so that they can also learn how to maximize their income, manage cash flow, and minimize stress in their freelance business.

Share your thoughts. Please share your thoughts about this book on X, Facebook, Instagram, LinkedIn, or any other of your favorite social media platforms, or write a book review and share it. It helps other people find *Finance for Freelancers* as well as my other books.

Amazon Author Page: https://www.amazon.com/stores/Veronica-Goldspiel/author/B0D466HRG9

Thank you! I can't wait to hear how *Finance for Freelancers* has helped your freelance business thrive and grow. Please write to me and let me know all about your successes! I look forward to hearing from you. You can contact me at Veronica@GoldspielCreativeEnterprises.com.

REMINDER

I also want to take this time to remind you about the FREE GIFTS I've created just for readers of this book.

FREE GIFTS JUST FOR YOU!

I've created some FREE GIFTS just for readers of this book. This FREE content contains some resources to help you more easily learn, grow, and succeed in your freelance career!

- **Freelancer's Resource & Tools Guide** – This is my list of books, audio, websites, and more to assist you in reaching your ultimate freelance career dreams.

- **The Freelancer's Life Private Facebook Group**: A vibrant community where freelancers unite to share insights, gain support, and elevate their careers. Whether you're just starting out or are a seasoned pro, join us to connect with like-minded professionals, discover success strategies, and thrive in your freelance journey. This is your space to learn, grow, and succeed together!

GET YOUR FREE GIFT NOW BY GOING TO:

https://goldspielcreativeenterprises.com/free-gifts-freelancer-success-sign-up/

CONNECT WITH ME ON FACEBOOK!

Join my *The Freelancer's Life* private Facebook community here:

https://www.facebook.com/groups/thefreelancerslife

ABOUT THE AUTHOR

Photo Credit: Dr. Alan Goldspiel

eronica Goldspiel, a #1 best-selling author and veteran freelancer with over two decades of experience, has worked with top motivational and self-improvement speakers worldwide, including luminaries like Tony Robbins and T. Harv Eker.

Veronica's expertise spans various sectors, from healthcare to entertainment, and offers a holistic approach to business and personal growth. Her extensive skills in social media management, content creation, and book publishing as well as health and wellness continue to empower clients globally.

As an author, Veronica penned works such as her #1 Best Sellers *Freelance Success Secrets: 21 Essential Habits That Will Transform Your Freelance Business from Surviving to Thriving*, *Dream Catchers: Mastering the Art of Realizing Your Dreams* and *From Likes to Profits: A Guide to Choosing the Most Profitable Social Media Platforms for Your Brand*. She also is the author of *Making Your Business a Social Media Superstar: A Step-by-Step Guide to Creating, Maintaining, and Promoting Your Online Presence*. Her commitment to sharing knowledge extends beyond books, as she regularly contributes to platforms like www.thefreelancerslife.com.

Driven by a passion for empowering others, Veronica focuses on producing books across her many areas of expertise to aid individuals in overcoming their challenges and to more easily achieve their aspirations. When she's not immersed in writing, Veronica can be found honing her barista skills with her espresso machine, engrossed in a good read, or enjoying beach outings with her husband, Alan.

You can connect with Veronica at: www.goldspielcreativeenterprises.com.

OTHER BOOKS BY AUTHOR

Freelance Success Secrets: 21 Essential Habits That Will Transform Your Freelance Business from Surviving to Thriving (The Freelancer's Life Series)

Reflections for Dream Catchers: The Inspirational Book of Wisdom for Your Journey to Success (Personal Growth and Motivational Series)

Dream Catchers: Mastering the Art of Realizing Your Dreams (Personal Growth and Motivational Series)

From Likes to Profits: A Guide to Choosing the Most Profitable Social Media Platforms for Your Brand (Small Business Wealth Marketing Series)

Making Your Business a Social Media Superstar: The Step-by-Step Guide to Creating, Maintaining, and Promoting Your Online Presence (as Veronica Buhl)

The Massage Disadvantage: What Doctors Know About Making Money That Massage Therapists Don't! (Co-Author as Veronica Buhl)

www.ingramcontent.com/pod-product-compliance
Lightning Source LLC
LaVergne TN
LVHW051835080426
835512LV00018B/2890